Meredith Corporation
100 Years *of* Publishing

Touch the soft fabric of any quilt made in the 20th century and the last thing that comes to mind is a printing press. Yet a printing press very likely played some role in the story of that quilt.

In the past 100 years, the print media have produced and distributed patterns, promoted styles, created broad public awareness, and united quilters, making what had been primarily a folk art into a more commercial and homogenized activity. At the same time, the increased exposure opened new opportunities for quilt writers, designers, entrepreneurs, and historians.

Meredith Corporation has played a prominent role in quilting's history, beginning with the company's first magazine, *Successful Farming*, launched in 1902 by Edwin Thomas, "E.T.," Meredith. Twenty years later, his idea for a publication for urban homeowners budded in *Fruit, Garden and Home*, which blossomed when the name changed to *Better Homes and Gardens*. Meredith's publishing venture grew into a multimedia giant, augmented in 1986 by the purchase of *Ladies' Home Journal*, for 103 years the leading magazine for women.

Combined, the pages of these three periodicals provide a distinct record that reveals the contributions made by quilt designers and the roles played by the two mass-circulation publishers who produced *Successful Farming*, *Better Homes and Gardens*, and *Ladies' Home Journal*. It is through these printed materials that researchers can now piece together the story of a century of quilts.

Contents

1902–1919

A New Century of Quilts   6

Quilters look to new and proliferating mass-circulation magazines for patterns and decorating ideas.

1920–1929

Roaring into the Twenties   22

From floral reproductions to artistic masterpieces, appliqué quilts are the rage.

1930–1939

A New Deal with Quilts

Times are tough and many quilters find comfort in creating quilts from pretty print and pastel fabrics.

Projects

1940–1969

The Middle Years

Dedicated crafters keep the tradition alive even though fabric selection is limited and quilting becomes less fashionable.

Projects

1970–2002

A Quilting Revival

America's Bicentennial celebration triggers a renewed enthusiasm for quilting in many shapes and forms.

Projects

Our Quilting Heritage

Mell Meredith

Heidi Kaisand

As Meredith Corporation begins its second century of operation, we will continue to provide information and inspiration for quiltmakers.

We're Proud of Our Past

In 2002, we celebrated a very special year here at Meredith Corporation, the company my great-grandfather founded. Our history, an American patchwork in itself, chronicles American life for 100 years. Since the first magazine we published, Meredith Corporation has been committed to providing our readers with meaningful information and inspiration. Even through turbulent times, our readers have steadfastly focused on what is important in their lives—family, friends, home, and creative expression. Our magazines and other products have reflected that commitment.

No example is lovelier, in my mind, than the varied ways our magazines have reflected and influenced the exceptionally rich history of quilting in this country. Whether it is stitched by hand or computerized sewing machine, a quilt is all about being inspired to create something special to share with others.

I hope you enjoy this treasury as much as I have. I am honored to work with the talented individuals who assembled this remarkable book. I know it will become another treasure in our archives as we enter our second century of publishing.

—Mell Meredith
Director, Corporate Planning, Meredith Corporation

A Look to the Future

Nothing has been more fascinating to me than learning about the lives and achievements of individual quiltmakers from the past. Truly ahead of their times, they provided a wealth of information about quilting in Meredith publications, reaching millions of people.

Meredith Corporation continues to play a crucial role in the history of quilting. With the publication of this special issue, *American Patchwork & Quilting*® has forged a link between the past and future of quilting. In this new century, we are dedicated to continuing our legacy of informing and inspiring quilters. It is with great excitement that we present this in-depth history of quilting through the years. I hope that by reading *Century of Quilts* you will be inspired to reminisce about your own quilting history, too.

—Heidi Kaisand
Executive Editor, *American Patchwork & Quilting*

Merikay Waldvogel

Xenia Cord

Susan Price Miller

A picture she discovered of designer Ernest Thompson Seton's elaborate appliqué quilt design in a 1905 issue of *Ladies' Home Journal* inspired **Susan Price Miller** to learn more about the connection between modern magazines and quilting. As project director and a writer for *Century of Quilts*, she defined that connection and provided in-depth profiles of the designers who established successful quilt businesses after exposure in mass-circulation magazines.

Susan's articles and quilting projects have appeared in *American Patchwork & Quilting,* and she has researched and written articles about Carlie Sexton and Hubert Ver Mehren for *Uncoverings*, the annual journal of the American Quilt Study Group.

Susan, an avid quilter and collector, also studies the history of quilts in the Netherlands and makes reproduction Dutch quilts.

Focusing on 20th-century quilt designers, events, and patterns, **Merikay Waldvogel** is a nationally known author, curator, and lecturer. Her passion for old quilts started in 1974 when a quilt in an antiques store window caught her eye. Merikay has written four books and numerous articles, including "A Collector's Clues to Dating Quilts" and "Tracking Down Quilts of the 1933 Chicago World's Fair."

After writing her second book, *Soft Covers for Hard Times: Quiltmaking and the Great Depression,* Merikay became an advocate for preserving magazine pages, brochures, catalogs, correspondence, and quilt kit packages. She currently serves on the Board of the Alliance for American Quilts, where she is developing the Boxes Under the Bed project to document quilt ephemera.

Merikay delved into her own extensive collection of 20th-century quilt patterns to write her chapters for *Century of Quilts*.

Interested in quilt history since teaching a graduate women's studies course on the subject in 1980, **Xenia Cord** specializes in researching vintage fabrics and 20th-century quilt kits and their manufacturers.

Xenia has presented and published articles in *Uncoverings* and has written numerous other historical articles which have been featured in such magazines as *American Patchwork & Quilting* and *McCall's Quilting*. She has also been a contributor to *The Twentieth Century's Best American Quilts: Celebrating 100 Years of the Art of Quiltmaking.* Currently she is researching a woman entrepreneur who marketed quilt kits in the 1920s.

Xenia contributed her expertise in historical fabrics and loaned swatches and quilts from her personal collection to be photographed for this book.

These dedicated historians combed past issues of Ladies' Home Journal, Successful Farming, Better Homes and Gardens, *and* American Patchwork & Quilting *to document the role Meredith publications played in the growth of quilting in America.*

In 1902 a young man in Des Moines, Iowa, founded a new publication—Successful Farming—to serve rural families throughout the country's heartland. E.T. Meredith, only 25 years old and the owner of a small Populist newspaper given to him as a wedding present by his grandfather, wanted his new monthly to discuss farm issues and present helpful information to farmers and their families. Within one year of publication, Successful Farming had 100,000 subscribers.

1902–1919
A New Century of Quilts

Launched in 1883, Ladies' Home Journal became so popular that by 1919, the magazine had more than 2 million readers.

FOR QUILTERS, POSSIBILITIES FILLED THE 20TH CENTURY. THE SEWING MACHINE PROVIDED A STREAMLINED WAY TO PIECE, AND FLOURISHING MASS-CIRCULATION MAGAZINES OFFERED PATTERNS TO COPY OR ORDER BY MAIL. LADIES' HOME JOURNAL LED THE WAY WITH DESIGNS FOR PRACTICAL, AS WELL AS ARTISTIC, QUILTS THAT WOULD BECOME FAMILY TREASURES.

ROBBING PETER TO PAY PAUL,
c. 1900; 83¾×91"

The beginning of the 20th century was a time of rapid transition in culture and society. Farmers were trading rural life for factory work in the cities, while new technologies were improving the lives of the growing middle class. Meanwhile, art and architecture reformers were rejecting the excessive Victorian styles, ostentatious displays of wealth, and the flood of impersonal, mass-produced goods. Instead, they favored simplicity and practicality—themes borrowed from the Arts and Crafts movement in England.

JOURNALIZING TURN-OF-THE-CENTURY STYLES

Ladies' Home Journal, based in Philadelphia, championed new looks for homes and furnishings and offered decorating advice for the bungalows and Prairie-style houses preferred by Arts and Crafts followers.

A simpler approach to living coincided well with the principles of the new field of home economics promoted by *Ladies' Home Journal*

Consistent with a simpler approach to living, two-color quilts were popular in the early 1900s.

and other women's magazines. Besides advocating built-in cabinets, sleeping porches, and modern kitchens as more efficient, easier to clean, and healthier, home economists also approved of the sanitary qualities of washable cotton quilts. Long-forgotten heirloom cotton quilts or newly made copies were said to complete stylish bedrooms.

Writers for *Ladies' Home Journal* from 1894 to 1907 applauded quilts carefully pieced from cotton fabrics in simple, geometric patterns restricted to white and one color, preferably red or blue, as shown in the blocks *above* and *left* and in the quilts, *opposite*. Deliberately chosen patterns and fabrics resulted in "effective" quilts of artistic merit. *Ladies' Home Journal*'s praise of this type of quilt undoubtedly influenced the making of two-color quilts in the early 1900s. (To make a two-color quilt, see *page 92*.)

Early Arts and Crafts proponents had made special efforts to return embroidery to a simpler style, too—one that they considered more artistic. This kind of "art needlework" first embellished the silk patches of late-19th-century crazy quilts. It continued through World War I in simpler form as outline designs

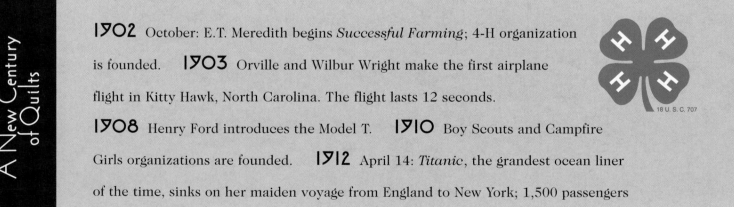

A New Century of Quilts

1902 October: E.T. Meredith begins *Successful Farming*; 4-H organization is founded. **1903** Orville and Wilbur Wright make the first airplane flight in Kitty Hawk, North Carolina. The flight lasts 12 seconds. **1908** Henry Ford introduces the Model T. **1910** Boy Scouts and Campfire Girls organizations are founded. **1912** April 14: *Titanic*, the grandest ocean liner of the time, sinks on her maiden voyage from England to New York; 1,500 passengers

18 U. S. C. 707

HONEYCOMB, 65×74", above left, and TREE OF LIFE, 51×76½", above right, are both done in indigo and white, two colors that were frequently paired in quilts at the turn of the century.

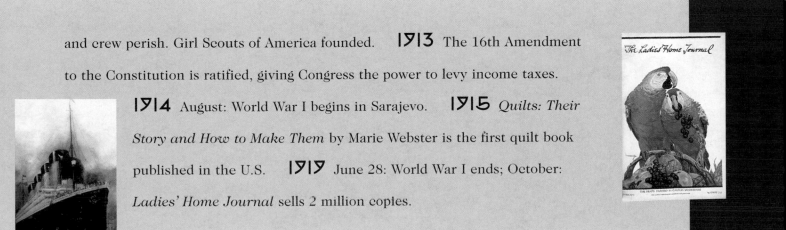

and crew perish. Girl Scouts of America founded.   1913 The 16th Amendment to the Constitution is ratified, giving Congress the power to levy income taxes.   1914 August: World War I begins in Sarajevo.   1915 *Quilts: Their Story and How to Make Them* by Marie Webster is the first quilt book published in the U.S.   1919 June 28: World War I ends; October: *Ladies' Home Journal* sells 2 million copies.

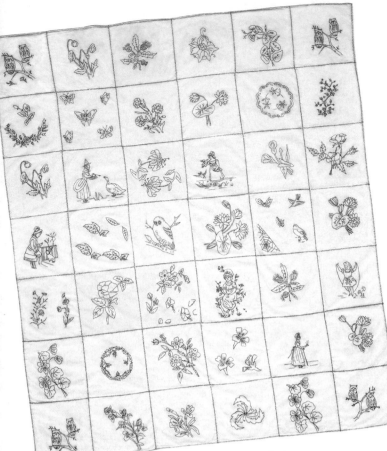

stitched in one color of thread, most often red but sometimes blue. Embroidery appeared on table and bed linens and almost anything made of plain fabric. Because colorfast Turkey red thread was the choice of many needleworkers, the embroidery became known as redwork.

Women created patterns by adapting pictures found in magazine ads and features. They also obtained collections of patterns and a stamping medium for transferring designs to fabric by mail order or as a free premium for new subscriptions. In the early years of *Ladies' Home Journal*, embroidery features and ads for supplies filled many pages.

SUCCESSFUL FARMING READERS SHARE HOMEMAKING TIPS

From its beginning, *Successful Farming* had "Farm Home Circle" pages devoted to the farm family. Features included paragraphs from readers, a poem, a photograph of an animal or children, recipes, mail-order garment patterns, and short articles. Farm wives shared ideas for saving time and making chores easier at a time when most farms had no electricity, running water, or central heat.

Several of the blocks of this redwork coverlet were embroidered using designs meant for linens from pre-1900 issues of Ladies' Home Journal. *Quilt patterns weren't published until after 1910. c. 1890; 62×72"*

LADIES' HOME JOURNAL BECOMES TRENDSETTER

Developments in the technology of printing at the end of the 19th century changed the publishing industry. The linotype machine, high-speed rotary presses, and the halftone method of reproducing photographs, plus the manufacturers' desire for national advertising, resulted in the modern mass-circulation magazine.

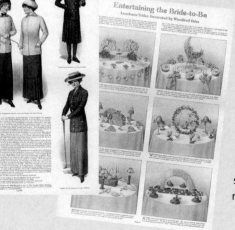

Cyrus Curtis, who founded *The Ladies' Home Journal* in 1883, was the first to see the opportunities these new technologies presented. Edward Bok, who became editor of *Ladies' Home Journal* in 1889, made the magazine one of America's top-selling publications for 30 years. He hired well-known writers, artists, and public figures as contributors; presented the latest styles in fashion, needlework, architecture, and interior design; advocated social reforms; and set the standards for taste.

Edward appealed to the growing urban middle class, especially to women with some leisure time and the income to purchase the expanding array of consumer goods. He and his staff dispensed information and advice in an intimate tone that made the magazine a fixture in the homes of devoted followers.

In the May 1905 issue, Ellen Cannady of Emporia, Kansas, suggested sorting the rag bag twice a year and saving linen and muslin for bandages, flannel for compresses, and old clothes for rag carpets. She recommended using leftover sewing scraps—not discarded clothing—specifically for quilts. "Pieces of dress goods, such as gingham, madras, or percale, should be saved until the dress is worn out, for they are often useful for mending them; after that they should be kept with the quilt pieces."

In January 1908, a reader shared how to prolong the life of a "comfort," which could be used for quilts too: "Baste strips of calico on the ends of comforts, and when soiled take off the strips and wash. The end becomes badly soiled oftentimes when the comfort otherwise is clean."

Ruth Forest's homemaking tip included in the September 1909 issue offered this advice: "Throw the bric-a-brac in the scrap pile and have less to clean and dust. Put in hard floors and banish carpets. Use an oil stove and quit melting over a hot range. Get simple meals for Sunday and quit making it a feast and work day. Take life easy for you will be a long time dead."

In November 1916, Mrs. L. M. G. praised the qualities of a white cotton blanket, which cost between 90 cents and $1, for use as a quilt interlining instead of batting. The blanket first needed to be preshrunk in boiling water, then blocked while drying. After that, "it quilts easily, washes well, is warm, light, easy to lay in place, and just as cheap as cotton batting."

CATALOGS SET FABRIC TRENDS

Vintage catalogs and swatch books of cotton fabrics that were used by manufacturers, wholesalers, and retailers such as Sears Roebuck & Co. are clues to the fabrics of the early 1900s. These publications recommended cottons for the informality of summer styles and "at home" wear, even among the most stylish elite.

In the 1890s and into the new century, color preferences ran to a warm pastel palette, which was softer than the darker shades of the 1880s. Lighter colors, involving white grounds with narrow shirting stripes, pastel plaids, even-weave or printed ginghams, sprigged calicoes, and solid chambrays in muted pastel shades were popular.

FUTURE QUILTERS OF AMERICA?

The former head of the Domestic Science Department at Iowa State College in Ames, Mrs. F. H. Waters began editing "Farm Home Circle" pages for *Successful Farming* in January 1911 and added longer articles of information and instruction. On the page specifically for "young housekeepers" that month, two drawings of a girl doing handwork were the subject of a contest. The first five correct responses explaining the correct sitting posture would win a year's subscription to the magazine. *Successful Farming* used many contests and promotions to keep reader loyalty and build circulation.

Which Position is the Correct One, and Why? The First Five Girls to Send in Correct Answer Will b Given a Year's Subscription to Successful Farming.

Plaids, even-weave ginghams, and prints were available to home sewers and quilters at the turn of the 20th century.

Dry Goods Catalogue Number 268, Fall & Winter 1916-17, left, distributed by Marshall Field & Co. of Chicago "for merchants only," offered several hundred cotton fabrics in solids and prints. Indigos, grays, chambrays, shepherd checks, shirtings, and double pinks for less than 10 cents per yard in standard goods, and "imperiale percales" for wrappers, housedresses, and men's shirts were shown in color. Designs included dots, mill engravings, diagonal plaids, stripes, even-weave checks, and florals. These were the fabrics of choice for home sewing, and the remnants often went into quilts.

Somewhat faddish prints appeared from season to season, notably black background cottons with hot, bright colors in idiosyncratic designs. In quiltmaking, certain combinations were favored, among them cadet blue, claret, and Shaker gray together, and white background shirtings with indigo or cadet blue. For the first two decades of the 20th century, a mixed palette of dark, serviceable cotton prints and light pastels in youthful designs also was available during this time.

Colorful fabric scraps left over from making Grandmother's print housedress or sewing Father's chambray shirt were destined for future heirloom quilts.

Quilters who ventured beyond two-color quilts had a variety of light and dark prints available to them in the early 1900s. Left: MONKEY WRENCH, c. 1900; 79¼×93½" Above: DOVE IN THE WINDOW, c. 1900; 89×109½"

An enterprising and practical quilter used the open spaces in this antique quilt for signatures. DELECTABLE MOUNTAINS, c. 1900; 90×98½"

APPLIQUÉ TAKES HOLD AT LADIES' HOME JOURNAL

A century ago, articles about quilts in *Ladies' Home Journal* were limited to patterns of fairly simple geometric designs and a few basic instructions about cutting and sewing.

In spite of the editors' early praise for pieced quilts above all other kinds, the appliqué style soon won the approval of readers and dominated *Ladies' Home Journal's* quilt features for many years. Two reasons may account for this. First, with appliqué, the forms and subjects were endless, so magazines could continually offer new and original designs to hold reader interest. Second, appliqué patterns were easy to provide for customers, either printed on paper for tracing or produced as iron-on transfers.

Selling these patterns was very profitable. In 1908, three years after the Home Pattern Co. was established to manufacture fashion and transfer patterns for *Ladies' Home Journal,* it employed 500 people and had sold 28 million patterns.

Magazine publishers offered quilt patterns and catalogs by mail order as a service to readers and to boost circulation.

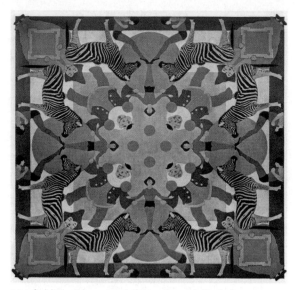

Maxfield Parrish created this unique quilt design. The original painting hangs in the Brooklyn Museum.

QUILTS AS ART

Ladies' Home Journal editor Edward Bok legitimized quilts as an art form by arranging for five leading artists and illustrators to design quilts for the magazine (see Maxfield Parrish's "A Circus Bedquilt," *above* and *opposite,* and two other commissioned designs on *page 16*). They created five illustrations reflecting their individual styles, all having complicated, detailed images requiring tremendous daring or skill on the part of anyone who tried to copy them in cloth.

All were appliqué designs; three used a strong medallion format. *Ladies' Home Journal* had intended to supply patterns for the quilts, but "practical obstacles" made it impossible.

Ernest Thompson Seton, an author and illustrator of wildlife books, produced the first illustration in January 1905, shown on *page 16*. In 1902, he had contributed a series of articles called "Ernest Thompson Seton's Boys" to *Ladies' Home Journal*. He fostered the national movement called Indian Scouts and later helped establish the Boy Scouts of America.

Ernest knew the fundamentals of making quilts. In his journal he described how his mother had made many quilts for her church in Canada and when she ran out of material for the filler, she used several sheets of newspaper "and quilted as usual. These quilts were extremely successful, warm and far more enduring than one might expect. The crackling of the papers wore out very early."

THE CIRCUS QUILT

Maxfield Parrish, a popular magazine and book illustrator, created one of the five artistic quilt designs commissioned by *Ladies' Home Journal* in the early 1900s. The Philadelphia native and New Hampshire resident had done work for the pages of *Ladies' Home Journal* before he won the competition to design the cover for the 250th issue in September 1904.

Maxfield created the design, shown *opposite*, for "A Circus Bedquilt" with zebras, clowns, and acrobats for the March 1905 issue. Though the design was printed in black and white, Parrish carefully prescribed the colors and warned they should be harmonious—either by using faded old clothes or dipping the finished piece in coffee.

As soon as quiltmaker Ada Luise Smith Hildner of Detroit saw "A Circus Bedquilt" in the magazine, she began to make the one shown *above* for her first child, a 2-year-old son, for Easter. She stitched in the corners of the 38×40-inch quilt: "Ernest G. Hildner Junior," "from Mother," "Easter" (which was April 23), and "1905." Ada had six more sons, but, as far as the family knows, made no other quilts.

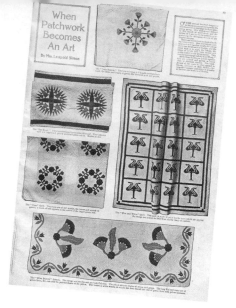

Less involved than the professional artists' quilts were Mrs. Leopold Simon's appliqué designs that appeared in Ladies' Home Journal *in 1908.*

The quilt Ernest designed for the magazine (see below, *left*), however, was unlike any other. In the square center panel, four antelope stood amid sagebrush in a Western landscape framed by multiple borders of sagebrush, jackrabbits, and snakes. Well-known animal characters from his books anchored the corners.

Another of the art quilt creators, Jessie Wilcox Smith, had worked for the *Ladies' Home Journal* advertising department before becoming a successful illustrator of books and magazines. Her "Child's Good-Night Bedquilt" (see below, *right*) depicted children preparing for bed circling the words of a poem from Robert Louis Stevenson's *Child's Garden of Verses*, which she was illustrating at the time.

Later, Mrs. Leopold Simon would provide another interpretation of quilting as an art in *Ladies' Home Journal*. In her August 1908 feature, *above*, "When Patchwork Becomes An Art," she commented on five antique quilt designs. She attributed the revival of interest in quilts "to the patriotic spirit governing the American women of the present century."

Writing in the context of the Colonial Revival style, popular at the time, she gave two of the patterns Colonial origins even though they were mid-19th-century designs. She did not explain why these quilts were art, although Arts and Crafts qualities were evident in the simple designs, cotton fabrics, and excellent handwork. Mrs. Simon provided no patterns but reviewed the basics of quilt construction.

The earliest appliqué patterns in <u>Ladies' Home Journal</u> were truly works of art—so complicated only accomplished quilters would attempt them.

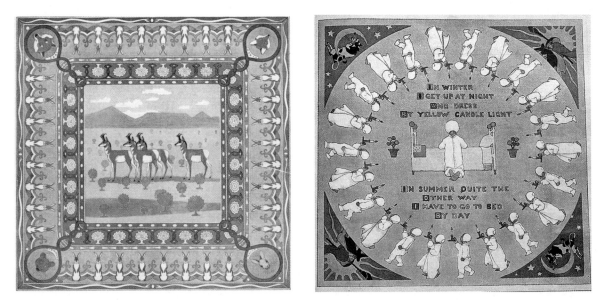

Editor Edward Bok legitimized quilting as an art by arranging for artists and illustrators to design quilts for Ladies' Home Journal. *Ernest Thompson Seton designed the quilt,* left, *and Jessie Wilcox Smith designed the bedtime quilt.*

In its January 1912 issue, Ladies' Home Journal featured the POPPY quilt by the most influential designer of the era, Marie Webster (see feature on page 19). c. 1915; 78×100"

QUILT COVERAGE DURING WORLD WAR I

Ladies' Home Journal had few references to quilts during the United States' involvement in World War I. However, a page of ideas for YMCA or Red Cross bazaars in the June 1917 issue included a tied baby carriage cover made with alternating light and dark squares of gingham and muslin.

During the war years, magazines focused on helping readers conserve goods and supplies rather than on artistic pursuits.

QUILTING FOR YOUR COUNTRY

An advertisement by the Rock River Cotton Company in the October 1919 issue of *Ladies' Home Journal* stated: "...the war taught American women many household economies, and revived the good old-fashioned practice of making quilts and comforters at home, as our grandmothers used to make them, of pure, fluffy cotton."

Editor Edward Bok decided that rather than send reporters abroad, *Ladies' Home Journal* would arrange for William Howard Taft of the Red Cross, Herbert Hoover of the Food Administration, and other heads of government departments to write columns about needs on the home front. Directions for canning food, stretching a dollar, and making items for servicemen dominated the magazine's pages.

A *Ladies' Home Journal* feature in February 1918 presented several home decorations: the latest quilt of popular designer Marie Webster (see feature, *opposite*), one of white baskets on a blue background; a simple "Rose Tree" quilt, also in appliqué; a silk boudoir couch cover; a "coach or automobile robe in Japanese silks"; and a "lounge or day-bed throw in cretonne with plain silk lining." An October suggestion to make a light, warm "comfort" for winter "by covering worn blankets with silkaline or cheesecloth and tacking together with worsted" underscored the need for economy.

At the same time, *Successful Farming* changed its editorial content to reflect its readers' focus on the war effort. Quilts went by the wayside as editors encouraged women to knit for the Red Cross, use substitutes for wheat, and conserve sugar, meat, fats, and even textiles. In December 1917, a reader described how she cut her husband's wool coats and trousers into squares and rectangles, then sewed the pieces together on the sewing machine to make comforters.

When the war ended in 1919, quilts returned to the pages of *Successful Farming* and *Ladies' Home Journal*. Mrs. T. R. wrote to *Successful Farming* to say she used up pieces of calico, gingham, and percale by cutting them into long pieces either 3 or 5 inches wide, then sewing pieces of the same width together in long strips. Once she determined the length of the quilt she wanted to make, she cut the sewn strips to match that measurement and sewed them together side by side, alternating the 3- and 5-inch-wide strips. All her stitching was done on the sewing machine.

Ladies' Home Journal's Premiere Quilter
Marie Webster

Color pages appeared in *Ladies' Home Journal* for the first time in 1910. The January 1911 issue took full advantage of color printing for a page of new quilts that changed the course of quiltmaking in the 20th century.

In "The New Patchwork Quilt," Marie Webster presented four quilts appliquéd in solid pastel colors. The description opened with the words, "A new and artistic note has been achieved in these designs for hand-made quilts of applied patchwork. The aim has been

to make them practical as well as beautiful by the use of colorfast linens of good quality in the patterns, and a foundation of equally good white muslin." These words clearly expressed the standards of the Arts and Crafts philosophy.

In her book *A Joy Forever: Marie Webster's Quilt Patterns,* Rosalind Webster Perry has written about how her grandmother's quilts reached the pages of *Ladies' Home Journal*. In 1909, the 50-year-old Marion, Indiana, woman wanted a quilt for her new Colonial Revival home. Having never made one before but skilled with a needle, she restyled a traditional appliquéd Rose of Sharon pattern in pastel linen. Family and friends urged Marie to send her beautiful "Pink Rose" quilt to the magazine. Editor Edward Bok immediately recognized the unique artistic qualities of the design and asked for more quilts from Marie for a full-page color feature, pictured *above*.

She turned to her flower garden for motifs for two more quilts, "Iris" and "Wind-Blown Tulip,"

and designed "Snowflake" for a third. The layout of "Pink Rose" resembled quilts of the 19th century, with repeating blocks, a grid scheme, and a swag border. The fabrics, soft colors, and undulating vinelike lines connecting the roses differentiated the quilt as something new. Marie's depiction of the irises and tulips in their natural forms was even more original.

Because her quilts were so popular with readers, Ladies' Home Journal published Marie Webster's designs for more than 15 years.

In short order, Marie also produced nine pillows with appliquéd flowers for the August 1911 issue, four more quilts for the January 1912 issue, and six crib-size quilts for the August 1912 issue. After delicately stitching down all the graceful shapes cut from solid-color fabrics and planning the elaborate quilting, she hired the residents at the Flinn Memorial Home in Marion to finish the handwork.

For her second series of quilts, Marie's use of poppies, morning glories, sunflowers, and dogwood blossoms arranged around a center motif hearkened back to the 19th-century medallion style. The graceful morning glories trailed in several bands while the bold sunflowers grew away from the binding, and the dogwood blossoms crisscrossed in lattice fashion, leaving open spaces in the middle for detailed quilting repeating appliquéd motifs.

Marie Webster

Because no patterns were available for the first series, readers' letters that had been mailed to the magazine were forwarded to Indiana, where Marie's family and friends pitched in to develop patterns. Her son had the idea to use blueprints for the patterns, and other family members cut full-size samples from tissue paper. The patterns, tissue samples, a sheet of instructions, and fabric swatches sold for 50 cents. *Ladies' Home Journal* produced 15-cent mail-order transfer patterns for four of the pillows, the "Morning Glory" and "Dogwood" quilts, and three of the baby quilts.

With the acceptance of her patterns in Ladies' Home Journal, Marie Webster was transformed from an Indiana wife and mother to a famous quilt designer.

Marie Webster's WREATH OF ROSES, 73×93", was published in October 1915. Unlike the original, the version above was made without a scalloped edge.

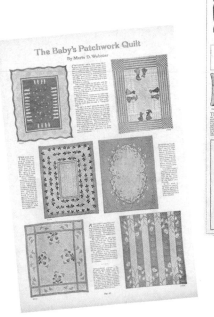

Left: *Marie Webster designed six crib quilts for the August 1912 issue.*

Not surprisingly, Marie became famous as a result of *Ladies' Home Journal* features. In 1912, Frank Doubleday, a publisher and friend of Edward Bok, asked her to write a book about quilts. She diligently traced the history of quilts and assembled a collection of photographs. Three years later, *Quilts, Their Story and How to Make Them*, the first book ever published about quilts, was greeted with rave reviews. Marie's designs directly influenced quilt styles for 20 years, and her book became a standard reference for generations of quiltmakers.

Even while researching and writing her book, Marie managed to design several more quilts, including the "Rose Quilt," better known as "Wreath of Roses," for *Ladies' Home Journal, left,* in October 1915. Variations on parts of the designs used separately on linens and cushions showed how patterns could be adapted for accessories. One variation on a chair back later became the "Wayside Roses" quilt. Her final quilt of the decade, "French Basket with Roses," appeared in February 1918. (To make pillows inspired by Marie's designs, see *page 88.*)

MORNING GLORY, c. 1920; 86×96"

The January 1912 issue of Ladies' Home Journal, *shown* left, *featured Marie Webster's* MORNING GLORY *quilt,* (top right) *and her well-liked* POPPY *quilt (top left),* shown on *page 17.*

In 1922, E. T. Meredith expanded his magazine lineup with Fruit, Garden and Home. *Two years later he changed the name to* Better Homes and Gardens.

1920–1929

Roaring into the Twenties

During the 1920s, Ladies' Home Journal *continued to grow, with a circulation far greater than other lifestyle magazines of the time.*

CAUGHT UP IN A CULTURE OF JAZZ, NEW FREEDOMS FOR WOMEN, AND ADVANCEMENTS IN TECHNOLOGY AND TRANSPORTATION, AMERICANS ENJOYED THE DECADE'S ECONOMIC GOOD TIMES. LEADING SUPPLIERS AND CREATORS OF QUILT PATTERNS CONTRIBUTED TO LADIES' HOME JOURNAL, SUCCESSFUL FARMING, AND THE NEW MAGAZINE FROM MEREDITH, BETTER HOMES AND GARDENS.

KALEIDOSCOPE,
c. 1925; 83×99"

In the 1920s, developments in transportation and communication rapidly changed society and created a common culture. The country became more united as people traveled by automobile, listened to the radio, talked on the telephone, and went to the movies. Urban and suburban areas spread out. More farmers moved off their land, lured by the attractions of the city and pushed by a post-war agricultural recession. At the same time, the remaining rural residents had better access to the same goods, services, and information their city cousins enjoyed.

MODERNISM AND THE COLONIAL REVIVAL

Art, architecture, and design reflected America's culture. Skyscrapers changed the urban landscape. In art, cubism, dadaism, surrealism, and abstract expressionism became major movements, and the style we now call Art Deco was simply called modern. The discovery of

King Tut's tomb in 1924 led to a craze for Egyptian design. Meanwhile, Colonial Revivalists looked to America's past for inspiration in decorating and handcrafts. While the wealthy built traditional two-story houses, young families bought smaller bungalows and decorated them with muslin curtains, rag rugs, and cotton quilts.

LIGHTER COLORS BRIGHTEN FABRICS

An abundance of pastel solids and multicolored small floral print fabrics fostered a growing interest in the "scrap" look that would come to dominate quiltmaking. (To make a table runner in pastel colors of the time, see *page 101*.)

Soft pink paired with green was popular for making appliqué quilts. Replicating classic quilt styles led to the reproduction of double pinks, green calicoes with tiny flowers, and yellow background calicoes. In solids, Turkey reds gave way to soft light reds, and pastel blues supplanted indigos and cadet blues.

Supple, lustrous cotton sateen was marketed in solid pastels. It was used extensively in whole-cloth and pieced quilts. Also new was rayon, which substituted for more expensive silk or satin whole-cloth boudoir quilts and occasionally found its way into pieced quilts.

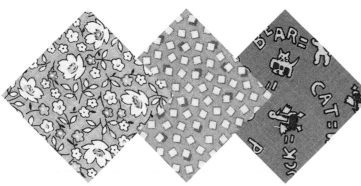

Small and floral prints and novelty fabrics, also known as conversation prints, were in vogue during the 1920s.

Roaring into the Twenties

1920 E. T. Meredith serves Woodrow Wilson's cabinet as Secretary of Agriculture; the 19th Amendment is ratified, giving women the right to vote; and Prohibition takes effect.   **1922** E. T. Meredith founds new magazine *Fruit, Garden and Home.*   **1923** The Charleston becomes a popular dance.   **1924** *Fruit, Garden and Home* name is changed to *Better Homes and Gardens.*

In the 1920s, quilters used the new pastel cotton fabrics to update mid-19th-century quilt designs that had been appliquéd in vivid reds and greens. TULIP QUILT, c. 1928; 82" square

"For old-fashioned quilts are the new-fashioned quilts, and there is no touch quite so modern in the present-day bedroom as that lovely relic of grandmother's time."
—*Ladies' Home Journal*, January 1922

1927 The Jazz Singer is the first talking movie; the first television transmission occurs; and Charles Lindbergh completes the first solo flight across the Atlantic in the *Spirit of St. Louis* airplane.

1929 Announcement of the first Academy Awards at a banquet at the Hollywood Roosevelt Hotel declares the movie *Wings* as movie of the year; the first car radio is produced; and the stock market crashes.

LADIES' HOME JOURNAL CHAMPIONS TRADITIONAL QUILTS

In January 1922, *Ladies' Home Journal* arranged an impressive color display of six fine vintage quilts for the article "Old-Time Patchwork and Appliquéd Quilts," *left*. The examples of the appliqué style outshone the simple red and white pieced basket quilt, which the magazine curiously turned into an appliqué project as well.

The article paid tribute to the creativity of American women, from Plymouth and Jamestown to isolated mountains and lonely plains, who made their own patterns and dyed their own cloth when necessary. "And there is no need to apologize for the humbleness of quilt making, for in the world of handicraft it has a high and honorable position," the editors said. No longer did the magazine equate quilts with

CHARLOTTE'S QUILT

A meticulous stitcher from Emporia, Kansas, Charlotte Jane Whitehill was inspired by the *Ladies' Home Journal* article shown *above*. She made her version of the 84×82" "Cherry Tree" quilt in 1936. The Denver Art Museum is home to "Cherry Tree" and 27 other Whitehill quilts.

Some of Charlotte's quilts illustrate the 1935 book *The Romance of the Patchwork Quilt in America*, by Carrie Hall and Rose Kretsinger.

art as it had a decade earlier. Nevertheless, women with the resources and time chose to make fine quilts to exhibit their needlework skills and good taste.

Ladies' Home Journal sold 75-cent transfer patterns for four of the featured quilts, including the pieced basket. The magazine publishers knew that using transfers for embroidery and appliqué designs had been a simple and successful method of providing patterns for sale by mail order, and the transfer method was so entrenched at the magazine that it was used for the pattern for the basket blocks. The 1922 pattern instructed readers to make the baskets by appliquéing the dark triangles on a white background, a difficult way to achieve precise geometric shapes.

SUCCESSFUL FARMING FEATURES HOME DECOR STORIES

With the end of wartime restrictions on the use of paper, publisher E.T. Meredith was free to print larger editions of *Successful Farming*. The influx of ideas from readers for sprucing up their home interiors suggests that farm women had a little more time and cash to invest in home improvement, at least before the farm economy began to suffer later in the decade. Several submissions featured directions for appliquéing conventional floral shapes onto plain muslin curtains, valances, and spreads in order to update farm homes.

FRUIT, GARDEN AND HOME DEBUTS

In 1921 when E. T. Meredith returned to Iowa after his stint as a Cabinet member in Washington, D.C., he revived his 10-year-old plans for a new publication. E. T. originally dreamed of a magazine focused on gardening and growing fruit, but he now envisioned a top-quality journal full of practical information and national advertising that would help families take care of their homes and yards.

The first issue of *Fruit, Garden and Home* came off the presses at Successful Farming Publishing in July 1922. Chesla Sherlock, recruited from the *Iowa Homestead* farm newspaper, came on board as editor. His enthusiasm, imagination, and inspirational writing embodied E.T.'s goals and gained readers' loyalty. E.T. frequently wrote his own column, "A Chat with the Publisher," and encouraged readers to send in their suggestions. In a short time, E.T. and Chesla agreed they would include "no fiction, no fashion; no piffle, no passion." They also had the policy that, no matter how interesting a feature might be, it would not be used if it did not tell how to do something.

In August 1924, E.T. changed the name of the magazine, which by that time had reached a circulation of half a million, to *Better Homes and Gardens*. Developments of small bungalows were making home ownership possible for middle-class families, and houses in the Colonial Revival style continued to be popular. People were buying, building, remodeling, decorating, and landscaping with a newfound fervor, and *Better Homes and Gardens* was their guidebook.

Having created a successful magazine for farmers, E. T. Meredith was ready to start a magazine for townspeople.

QUILT DESIGNERS MAKE THEIR MARK

In the realm of handwork, *Successful Farming* introduced the work of three women in three successive months at the end of 1922. Two of the three, Emma Shackelford Tyrrell and Carlie Sexton, were native Iowans. Both developed their hobbies into crafts and quilt features for several farm and home magazines published in Des Moines. The third woman, Ruby Short McKim, was a trained designer from Missouri who already had a national reputation for her distinctive embroidery designs. (For more information about these women, see the personal profiles beginning on *page 31*.)

After the birth of Better Homes and Gardens, designers who had appeared in Successful Farming began contributing to Meredith's new magazine.

At the end of the 1920s, all three responded to a growing interest for quilt information and patterns by the readers of *Better Homes and Gardens*. Their features reassured busy women that they could make quilts in the style of their grandmothers or in the newest fashion.

As the fall of 1929 began, *Successful Farming* found a new designer who would bring original designs to quilt, rug, pillow, and other crafts projects to Meredith magazines for five years. Laura Holmes, a graduate of the Art Institute of Chicago teaching at the University of Wisconsin, wrote about hooked rugs for her first *Successful Farming* feature in

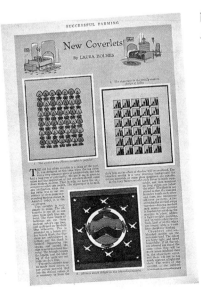

September 1929. (To make a felted wool project adapted from her design, see *page 97*.)

A month later she switched to coverlet motifs as shown *below left*. Two reflected themes of modern life: the tall buildings of a city skyline and submarine, steamship, and airplane transportation. "Fairy Flower," the third coverlet, *top left*, lined up rows of rounded shapes colored in soft pastels and had a more delicate appearance. Although the article did not specifically instruct readers to do so, these tops could have been layered with batting and backing and stitched into quilts.

MARIE WEBSTER RETURNS TO LADIES' HOME JOURNAL

Just as *Better Homes and Gardens* and *Successful Farming* contained more sustained information about quilting beginning in 1927, *Ladies' Home Journal* published a new Marie Webster design—the first in almost 10 years. (For more information about Marie, see *page 19*.) For the woman who did not have a quilt from her grandmother, the September 1927 issue of *Ladies' Home Journal*, *above*, suggested a solution in "Pink Dogwood in Appliqué for the Bedroom." Quilters could order transfer pattern No. 643 for 60 cents, cut out fabric pieces, turn under the edges, and "the rest is merely a matter of hemming and running stitch." The feature focused on having a quilt "without too much labor or too much money outlay either." Patterns were available from the Practical Patchwork Company, which was started by Marie and two friends in Marion, Indiana, in 1921. The women also sold kits, basted tops, and handmade quilts.

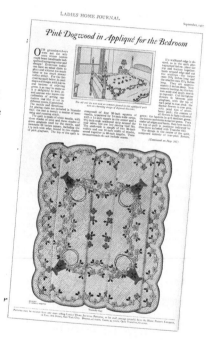

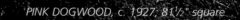

PINK DOGWOOD, c. 1927, 81½" square

Despite the dominance of magazine articles about appliqué quilts, quilters continued to piece quilts such as this variation of TUMBLING BLOCKS. c. 1920; 70×72"

Meredith's Dynamic Designers
Ruby Short McKim

In December 1922, *Successful Farming* debuted the first contribution by Ruby Short McKim. She was a professional designer who had studied at a New York art school and taught classes for the Independence, Missouri, schools. Ruby's innovative ideas for all kinds of needlework and home-decorating projects reached a wide audience through the pages of *Successful Farming* in the 1920s and led her to become an editor at *Better Homes and Gardens* in 1928.

Ruby had a talent for capturing a character with a few essential lines. In 1916, she drew some squared-off Art Deco-style figures for the *Kansas City Star*. These designs, intended for outline embroidery on quilt blocks and commonly known as "Quaddy Quilties," may be the earliest-known quilt pattern series published in a major newspaper. She syndicated over 20 other embroidery and quilt pattern series in the next 20 years.

In 1917, Ruby married Arthur McKim. They settled in Independence, Missouri, where Arthur ran their mail-order business for products designed by his wife.

Ruby submitted five features to *Successful Farming* from 1922 to 1928. Most included actual-size designs for embroidery on linens, clothing, and gifts. For example, the reader could trace a pair of "greedy geese" in Ruby's geometric style or a fat rooster in her curvy "Roly Poly" style onto a baby bib or an apron pocket. She also created a stylized butterfly and flower for "country mothers" who "wield a brush for beauty" to paint on flowerpots, boxes, and cans. Ruby sold transfer patterns for the first time in her November 1928 article for *Successful Farming*.

Ruby Short McKim was a designer for Meredith magazines for more than a decade.

Enthusiastic embroiderers looked forward to seeing Ruby Short McKim's full-size patterns in the pages of *Successful Farming*. Readers could send in a self-addressed, stamped envelope and receive a free sheet of carbon paper for tracing the designs.

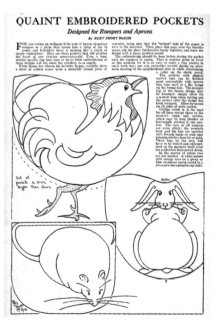

Ruby Short McKim

Ruby's career reached a new plateau in January 1928, when she began writing the "Adventures in Home Beautifying" column for *Better Homes and Gardens*. The bathroom was the first of a series of rooms to receive the benefit of her decorating ideas and designs for accessories. She included an alphabet of graceful initials for embroidery on linens. She also offered splashing fish motifs to stencil on a wall border or shower curtain or to hook into a round rug. The quality of the designs and easy how-to directions set a high standard for the magazine's decorating stories.

Ruby's full-size patterns appeared in the Kansas City Star beginning in 1928.

Each month Ruby focused on a different room of the house, including the sunroom and sleeping porch. In September 1928, she gave decorating tips for brightening a north-facing room. Her suggestions included a yellow and turquoise color scheme and organdy curtains featuring shadow-appliqué tulips across the

hem and the valance. Her artful plans were overshadowed, however, by her original Art Deco-style quilt blocks splashed across the page. These geometric pieced patterns added an entirely new concept to the quilt world. Instructions and cardboard patterns could be ordered for 20 cents each, or all three for 50 cents.

Once Ruby covered all the rooms in a house, she devoted each monthly feature to decorating with craft projects using coordinating designs. Her purpose is best summed up by the words "Expressing Yourself in Your Home," the title of the February 1929 article that included another original quilt block called Nosegay. This collection of appliquéd flowers clustered above a basket of eyelet fabric was in response "to many requests for a lovely new quilt design in appliqué."

A few months earlier, on September 19, 1928, her full-size pattern pieces for the traditional Pine Tree quilt block from McKim Studios appeared in the *Kansas City Star* newspaper. This was the beginning of a 33-year offering of full-size quilt patterns by the paper. The popular series, known to quilters and pattern collectors today as *Kansas City Star*

> "The exhibition coverlet these days is ever so often a quilt; bedspreads are experiencing competition to maintain their positions on top. For beds of quaint or unpretentious type, the quilt is certainly logical."
>
> —Ruby Short McKim
> *Better Homes and Gardens*
> October 1929

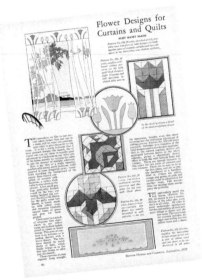

The blocks of GEOMETRIC ROSE, *left, are based on a Ruby McKim pattern featured in the September 1928 issue of* Better Homes and Gardens, *shown above.*

patterns, was and is beloved by quilters. The clippings from the *Kansas City Star* newspaper are hoarded, traded, and bought and sold even today. Ruby supplied many of the patterns until September 20, 1930, after which staff illustrator Eveline Foland took over.

In her October 1929 feature for *Better Homes and Gardens* magazine, Ruby introduced two series of 12 or more full-size patterns collected into 15-cent booklets titled "Patchwork Patterns," shown *left*. Some of the patterns had been published in the *Kansas City Star*. Ruby's remark "that hundreds of you sent for our pieced flower blocks last fall" indicates that reader response may have prompted her to prepare several collections of common patterns.

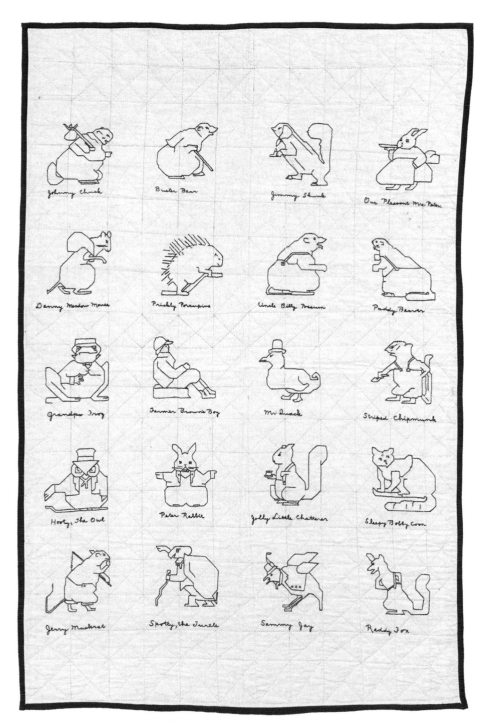

Ruby Short's first designs for embroidered quilt blocks were based on characters from Thornton Burgess's Bedtime Stories. *The Kansas City Star published them in 1916, a year before Ruby married Arthur McKim. Turkey red thread was still the color of choice for outline embroidery, although blue became more common in the 1920s. BEDTIME QUILT, also known as QUADDY QUILTIES, c. 1920; 36×55"*

Meredith's Dynamic Designers
Emma S. Tyrrell

Emma Shackelford grew up in the rural Elkhart area near Des Moines. She taught school before becoming one of the first registered nurses in Iowa and marrying Dr. Joseph W. Tyrrell. A multitalented woman who could write well, Emma also crocheted, quilted, made soft toys, and collected buttons.

Emma's first article for *Successful Farming* in November 1922 encouraged mothers to make stuffed animals and dolls for Christmas gifts. Full-size patterns were available for readers who sent in enough stamps to cover the 4 cents due for return postage. Clearly these patterns were a service for subscribers and not a moneymaker for the magazine or the creator.

Emma put together three more toy collections for late-year issues. Her November 1927 article was something entirely different, however. "We Copy Grandmother's Quilting," shown *left*, told knowingly and lovingly of old quilts, the craft of assembling a quilt, and the art of quilting. She wrote: "To our great-great-grandmothers the pieced quilts were the pick-up work for all spare moments, while the patched [appliquéd] quilts were their especial pride and delight. No wonder that they were fine characters, with quilt-piecing to teach them patience and to give them time to meditate and invite their souls."

Emma went on to attribute the revival of interest in old needlework and quilts to the popularity of Colonial furniture. With nostalgia she inspired her readers to follow the methods of marking a top, putting it on a large frame, and making tiny running stitches by hand. The article also showed some 10-cent quilting patterns readers could order and announced the publication of a booklet containing a larger collection of Emma's favorite designs. The inspirational sentiments and practical information alone made *Successful Farming*'s mail-order catalog, "Old-Time Quilting Patterns," *right*, well worth the 10-cent price.

In January 1929, Emma proved herself a thoroughly modern quilt designer who took great care in her work. Inspired by Lindbergh's solo flight across the Atlantic Ocean, she designed her "Lone Eagle" quilt after consulting a pilot about the correct proportion and details. Airplane blocks, which could be either pieced or appliquéd, alternated with plain squares quilted with an eagle motif.

> *Emma Tyrrell would collaborate with Ruby Short McKim on many quilting articles for Better Homes and Gardens in the 1930s.*

> **"O**ld quilts are now among the treasures of the household. Even today when women are in far too many activities to do fancy work we find them still eager for quilting designs."
> —Emma Tyrrell, *Successful Farming* January 1929

"Quilting is more than a pastime. It is an art, an art with a growing fascination. After working out one design, we are tempted to do another, and another, until quilting has become a hobby. And why not? It is a most worthy means of self-expression..."

—Emma Tyrrell,
Successful Farming
November 1927

Emma's most famous design is the LONE EAGLE, c. 1930; 75×85". The unknown quiltmaker followed Emma's suggestions for the color scheme but highlighted the eagles with embroidery instead of quilting them in the plain setting squares.

> "*I* wish you who love the old quilts as I do could come with me on some of my little rambles, for there are lovely old covers in every locality but many are hidden away, unknown and sometimes unloved. When I visit in a home and talk with a grandmother who really has done much quilting I feel my time is well spent, for quilt people are generally homey people. They like flowers and pretty colors. So do I, and our little chats are always happy."
> —Carlie Sexton, *Better Homes and Gardens,* February 1927

DEMOCRATIC ROSE, c. 1929; 69×78"

Meredith's Dynamic Designers
Carlie Sexton

The third woman introduced in *Successful Farming* was Carlie Sexton. She was a fourth-generation quilter, raised by an aunt who had won many blue ribbons for her quilts at the Iowa State Fair. For years, Carlie supervised the clerical staff at *People's Popular Monthly*, another Des Moines periodical. When the *Monthly* needed articles about quilts, she wrote them because she was the only one on staff who knew anything about the subject. A note at the end of her second column announced that she would provide patterns for five different blocks at 10 cents each. At age 45, Carlie launched her career as a mail-order entrepreneur with nothing more than a typewriter, a mimeograph machine, and a love for quilts.

Carlie wrote *Successful Farming*'s first full-page quilt feature in January 1923, shown *below*. Photographs of her "Wreath of Roses" quilt and seven individual quilt blocks illustrated the article "Old-Time Patchwork Quilts." In her casual, personal style, she wrote: "With the return of poster beds, braided rugs, and muslin and chintz curtains, the patchwork quilt is almost a necessity, and many of the old patterns are being reproduced in the new and softer shades."

Carlie interwove comments about each pattern with tidbits of history and suggestions for suitable fabrics. The article coincided with the publication by Successful Farming Publishing Company of her catalog, also titled "Old-Time Patchwork Quilts."

One of the first suppliers of printed patterns, Carlie gave the names Indiana Rose, Iowa Rose, and Ohio Rose (left to right) to these blocks.

A prolific writer and founder of a successful mail-order pattern business, Carlie Sexton also wrote quilting books.

She later claimed that she had filled all the orders for books and patterns herself and added the customers' names to her mailing list. This exposure in a magazine with a circulation approaching 1 million certainly gave her pattern business a tremendous boost.

Carlie's only feature for *Better Homes and Gardens*, "Quilts We Rarely See," appeared in February 1927. Two years earlier, Carlie had visited a friend in southeast Iowa, taken pictures of many old quilts, and written down their stories. The magazine published photographs of "Democratic Rose," "Aunt Dinah's Delight," "Grapes and Morning-Glory," and five other quilts. Carlie wrote, "Don't these old quilts just seem to open the door to romance? From the fragrant gardens our great-grandmothers grew, it is not much wonder they designed the rare and beautiful old patterns that are real works of art."

While Better Homes and Gardens *focused on home and family,* Ladies' Home Journal *acknowledged that its primary goal was to entertain readers.*

1930-1939

A New Deal with Quilts

In March 1931, an illustrated quilt appeared on the cover of Successful Farming. *Though quilting was not a regular feature in the magazine during the 1930s, original and syndicated patterns were frequently offered for sale.*

WITH THE GREAT DEPRESSION, THE DUST BOWL, AND WAR IN EUROPE MAKING AMERICANS FEEL VULNERABLE, QUILTING SURGED FORWARD AS A CRAFT OF NECESSITY, RATHER THAN LUXURY. NATIONAL MAGAZINES BROUGHT HAPPINESS AND HOPE TO THEIR READERS AND FEATURED QUILTING AS A PRACTICAL, ECONOMICAL, AND ENJOYABLE CRAFT.

Because patterns for GRANDMOTHER'S FLOWER GARDEN were widely distributed in the 1930s, this quilt has become an American classic. c. 1935; 85½×91"

Called the good old days by some, the decade of the 1930s is etched in our national memory. The images of hardship are vivid—of businessmen selling apples on street corners, families heading west in old jalopies, and children working in dangerous conditions.

But the 1930s were also heady times. Franklin Delano Roosevelt became president. Passenger trains traveled coast to coast, carrying tourists to national parks and world-class expositions in Chicago, San Francisco, and New York City. Stifling Prohibition ended, and the movie industry was in its heyday: Walt Disney's first feature-length cartoon, *Snow White and the Seven Dwarfs,* opened in 1937, and *Gone with the Wind* debuted in 1939.

New appliances and electricity reached most neighborhoods, making homemaking and cooking easier. Nightly radio broadcasts brought the family together. Even unwired homes received broadcasts on battery-powered sets. Commercial stations featuring music from the Metropolitan Opera to the Grand Ole Opry clamored for more listeners and advertisers.

Inspiring magazine articles, upbeat radio shows, and escapist movies lifted the spirits of folks through hard times.

QUILTING KEEPS GROWING

Women in the 1930s quilted, even though most of them used a sewing machine and could purchase inexpensive bedspreads at department stores. When they were forced to enter the workplace as the economy crashed, women still found time for handwork.

Magazine publishers, attuned to the appeal of quilts as well as the needs of their readers, adapted and updated quilt designs. Writers paired the themes of "old" and "new" in the text they wrote describing each quilt. Pattern designers used antique quilts for inspiration but also produced modern quilt projects in colorful fabrics to coordinate with the latest home-decorating trends.

Quilting-related products became a major industry, and quilt product advertisers sold all sorts of laborsaving devices (precut templates, die-cut pieced quilt kits, stamped embroidery blocks, and perforated quilting patterns) to entice the quilter with little time.

At the depths of the Great Depression, with most families' incomes limited and their resources stretched, more than 24,000 quilters entered a national contest sponsored by Sears Roebuck & Company. Organized to coincide with the 1933 Chicago World's Fair, the contest may go on record as having the most quilts ever submitted. With materials costing less than $5 to make a bed-size quilt, the chance of winning $1,000 was likely a powerful motivation for many entrants.

A New Deal with Quilts

1930 *Better Homes and Gardens* introduces its *Cookbook* designed as a loose-leaf notebook. **1932** Franklin Delano Roosevelt is elected president during the Great Depression. **1933** *Ladies' Home Journal* celebrates its 50th anniversary; Singer Sewing Machine Co. introduces the Featherweight sewing machine at the

Pastels and prints continued to be popular fabrics for quilts in the 1930s.
DOGWOOD, c. 1938; 83×83"

Chicago World's Fair; Prohibition ends. **1934** The Dionne Quintuplets are born in Canada. **1935** *The Romance of the Patchwork Quilt in America*, by Carrie Hall and Rose Kretsinger, is published. **1936** The Golden Gate Bridge in San Francisco is completed. **1937** The first feature-length Disney movie, *Snow White and the Seven Dwarfs*, premieres. **1939** Major motion pictures *Gone with the Wind* and *The Wizard of Oz* are released; September 1: Germany invades Poland.

In March 1933, Successful Farming *editors featured this quilt pattern made from an array of the "new gay designs and colors of the day." TRIP AROUND THE WORLD, c. 1935; 87×98"*

Novelty cotton prints featured Disney characters from popular animated films.

NEWFANGLED FABRICS

Although the frugality of the Depression sometimes decreased the quality of goods produced at the time, cotton fabrics appear to have been little affected. Manufacturers and distributors stressed style, value, and quality in their lines, continuing to show the same sorts of florals, stripes, shirtings, Shaker grays, and novelties that had been staples in the 1920s. Colors remained bright and cheerful, with pastels yielding to warmer shades and floral prints growing bolder in size and hue. (To make two quilts in 1930s reproduction prints, see *pages 104 and 108*.) Orange was a strong color and was often paired with turquoise or brown. Pink and lighter blues were less commonly shown, except in standards such as solids, gingham checks, or shirting stripes, where they were used as background colors. Toward the end of the decade, there was a move toward rich, dark backgrounds like chocolate brown, magenta, turquoise, and even black—all with bright colors overlaid.

Novelty designs, especially for children, featured animals, modes of transportation, fairs and circuses, and tiny figures at play. Disney Studios marketed popular character fabrics in the wake of its box office successes, showing *Snow White and the Seven Dwarf*s in several color combinations. These novelties were used in feed-sack designs later in the decade of little girls at household chores, boys at play, animals, fruits and vegetables, buildings, and common objects. During the decade, there were several popular color trends, perhaps none more lasting than orchid, green, and gold in combination.

In textile sample books throughout the 1930s, fabrics in strong lavender, orchid, and bright yellow hues with green and gold accents appeared, sometimes with turquoise replacing the green or with orange instead of gold. Toward the end of the decade the florals became larger and more impressionistic in appearance. Backgrounds were dark, and the overall effect appeared to be more for home decoration than for personal sewing or quiltmaking.

Even with the uncertain economy of the Depression, quilters could find plenty of colorful cotton fabrics in cheery prints.

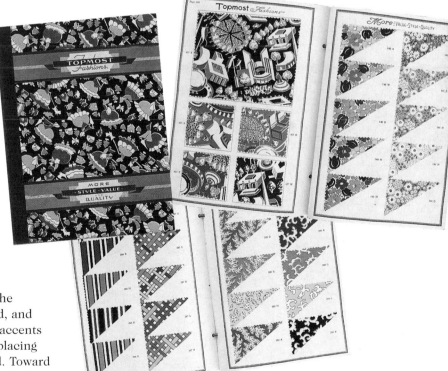

Manufacturers promoted their newest colors and designs by sending swatch books, such as this one from 1938, to their retailers.

In the 1930s, quilting articles continued to be an important part of Successful Farming magazine.

QUILTS FOR FARM WOMEN

In 1930, Meredith published "Yesterday's Quilts in Homes of Today," Carlie Sexton's latest little book about quilts and their stories. (For more information about Carlie, see *page 37.*) An advertisement in *Successful Farming*'s January 1931 issue called it a "NEW booklet about OLD quilts."

Laura Holmes, who followed Carlie at *Successful Farming*, suggested her readers combine their love of quilts with history and take advantage of the bicentennial of George Washington's birthday in planning their annual fall bazaars. In the October 1932 issue shown *left*, she wrote, "Make your bazaar an exhibition as well as a sale. Display your heirlooms—antique furniture, samplers, dresses, quilts and rugs. Dress booth attendants and children in patriotic costumes. Have special booths showing various American crafts, such as hooking and quilting. Have beautiful examples of old quilts for inspiration. Have as many quilt block designs as you can collect cut from wrapping paper, all ready to sell. Show a finished block of each quilt. There should be a great demand for these."

FEED-SACK FRENZY

In the mid-1920s, Gingham Girl Flour was sold in red-and-white gingham bags, perhaps the first time that reusable print fabric appeared as packaging for items such as flour, sugar, salt, grains, seeds, and feed. Husbands who bought feed or seeds in 98-pound sacks were admonished by their wives to search for matching bags, as it took four bags, measuring approximately 36×42 inches when opened, to make a woman's dress.

Designs ranged from small florals to bold plaids, stripes, novelty designs, and figures in vivid, sometimes garish colors and combinations. Feed sacks came in at least five fabric qualities, some with a lower thread count than domestic yard goods. But the fabric was serviceable for everything from clothing and kitchen curtains to slipcovers and quilts. For the next 40 years, printed cotton bags, commonly called feed sacks, were a staple for home sewing, especially in rural areas.

SNAIL'S TRAIL, c. 1930–1940; 69½×80"

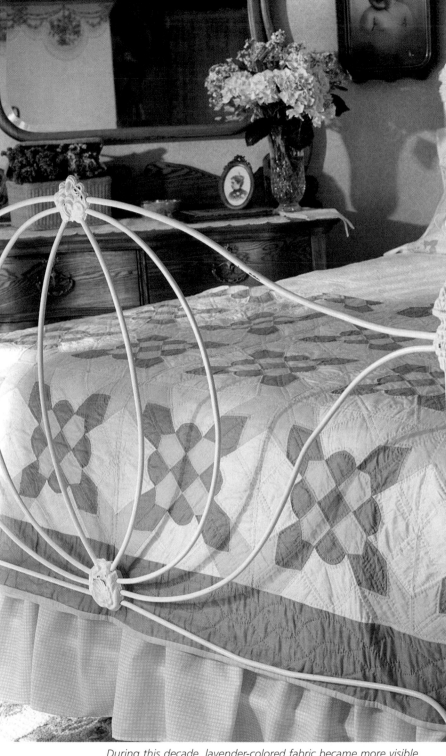

During this decade, lavender-colored fabric became more visible in quilts and was often combined with yellow. FULL BLOWN TULIP, c. 1935; 72×90½"

The quilting cotton with the soft, glazed surface, through which it is so easy to push a needle, was perfected just about six years ago. It may be in part responsible for the present widespread quiltmaking vogue, since it has certainly simplified the most tedious part of the operation—quilting."

—*Better Homes and Gardens*, April 1934

DOUBLE WEDDING RING,
c. 1934; 80×90"

Florence La Ganke Harris, writing the "Nancy Page Quilt Club" newspaper column, was Ruby Short McKim's main competition during the late 1920s and early 1930s. Florence wrote "Spreading Beauty" in the December 1935 issue of *Successful Farming*, shown *below*. The article featured a photograph of bedspreads and quilts she designed. She wrote, "The modern feeling in these designs fits in with new furniture. Based on classical motifs, as these are, they do not quarrel with eighteenth-century fittings and their adaptability adds to their charm." She also suggested, "if greater masculinity is demanded, try changing the fabrics and color. For example, The Festoon Design with its brown background and white festoons and stars is made seemingly for a man's room. But if three shades of lavender are used, they could be put on an eggshell background and result in a spread that is as feminine as the latest note in fashions." The feature was so popular that her patterns continued to be sold long after the article appeared.

In the December 1939 issue of *Successful Farming*, Fleeta Brownell Woodroffe, a well-known gardening writer from Iowa, was introduced to readers as a quilt authority. According to the information beside her photograph, "Mrs. Woodroffe is as skillful a quilter as she is a flower-grower."

In her article "Like to Quilt?" Fleeta proved her quilting sensibilities. She offered tips for beginners: "Be as modern as you like. Plan for a good border. Use 'Sunbonnet Sue' as a memory quilt, making each dress with scraps from your friends' and classmates' dresses and shirts." She also predicted, "The quilts of 1940 are going to be as lovely to touch as to look at. Never were colors so good or fabrics so pleasant to work on as today."

Like other magazines of the time, Successful Farming showed quilt designs, but readers had to order patterns by mail.

Above: *Hubert Ver Mehren (see feature on page 54) sold the patterns which were illustrated in Fleeta Woodroffe's article. The second block from the left is the popular "Double Wedding Ring."*

Spreading Beauty
By Florence La Ganke Harris

A syndicated quilt columnist, Florence La Ganke Harris had only one article, above, published in Successful Farming.

"There's something about quilts that never grows old; the quilt, yes, but never the fascination of seeing beauty grow under your fingers. A patch a day adds up to a quilt by and by. You never think, even once, about its being a big job."

—Fleeta Brownell Woodroffe, *Successful Farming*, December 1939

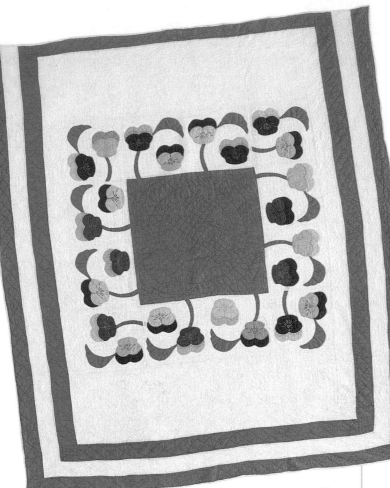

RUBY SHORT McKIM'S MAIL-ORDER MAGIC

When Ruby Short McKim moved from *Successful Farming* to *Better Homes and Gardens* in 1928, she was already a renowned quilt designer due to her nationally syndicated patterns. (For more information about Ruby, see *page 31*.) In 1931, she published *One Hundred and One Patchwork Patterns*, a compilation of her syndicated quilt patterns, which she and her husband sold through mail order.

Ruby's articles in *Better Homes and Gardens* in the early 1930s often contained the same illustrations and text descriptions of quilt patterns and quilting templates that appeared in her mail-order catalog, *Designs Worth Doing*. Although readers were directed to order the products from Ruby Short McKim at the *Better Homes and Gardens* Des Moines post office box, the inquiries were probably forwarded to and supplied by McKim Studios in Independence, Missouri.

Clever design coupled with simplified construction epitomizes the high standards Ruby set for herself and her products. The "Pansy" quilt, c. 1930, shown *above left*, measured 72×84 inches and was sold as a pattern for 25 cents, as a kit with 8⅔ yards percale for $3.35, or as a kit with 8⅔ yards sateen for $5. The transfer quilting design cost 20 cents, and the cable, feather, and pineapple perforated patterns cost 25 cents each.

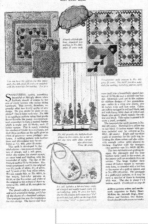

Other than titling the article "Quilts—We Never Have Too Many" and adding two new lead-in sentences, Ruby's choice of words in the March 1930 issue of *Better Homes and Gardens* is exactly the same as the description in her catalog, *Designs Worth Doing,* also published in 1930.

"Something useful, something beautiful or fittingly clever when finished should of course be the aim of every woman who enjoys doing handwork," advised Ruby.

Her "Pansy" quilt, shown *above*, is described as "...an appliqué pattern using that gentle favorite the pansy, conventionalized somewhat to form a central border which is really just twelve blocks, each 12 inches square."

One Hundred and One Patchwork Patterns

Ruby's only book of patterns is still available today—70 years after it was first published.

THE CITY GIRLS' MAGAZINE

In the 1930s, *Ladies' Home Journal*, whose readers primarily lived in cities, featured far more short stories, fashion and beauty features, and party planning and decorating tips than articles about home sewing and quiltmaking.

The editors of *Ladies' Home Journal* rarely if ever alluded to the bleak outlook of the early 1930s, with one exception. In "The Hostess" column published in the June 1931 issue, shown *right*, the editor described a curious solution to the hard times:

"There has been a fad the past winter for giving Poverty Parties. So many people have felt it wise to cut down unnecessary expenses this year, that a number of clever hostesses decided to feature this temporary leanness of pocketbook, and use it as the basis for a new, jolly type of party.

"Hostess and guests all wear their oldest clothes, the menu is simple to the point of being amusing, you don't play cards for prizes, and often the lunch, tea or supper, whichever it may be, is served in picnic style, with either your oldest crockery or real paper picnic plates."

Maybe not so surprising, given *Ladies' Home Journal*'s history and urban audience, was the fact that only three quilt-related articles appeared in the magazine in the 1930s.

Because Ladies' Home Journal chose to focus more on fashion and entertaining, quilting articles appeared rarely during the 1930s.

THE "BIBLE QUILT"

Although quilting was not regularly featured in *Ladies' Home Journal*, in August 1938, the magazine featured the "Bible Quilt" designed as a bedtime story for children. The editors explained, "...each square is a different story. Ask your own child the title of the picture—Daniel and the Lions, the Parting of the Red Sea, Noah's Ark, and Jonah and the Whale." The 12 drawings were printed on large sheets of paper, and colors and fabrics were suggested. They cautioned, "It will take some time to make this quilt!" Little is known about the designer of the "Bible Quilt," although the format is similar to Marion Cheever Whiteside's "Story Book Quilt" patterns, which did not appear in *Ladies' Home Journal* until the 1940s. (For more information about Marion, see *page 68*.)

Chicago resident Bertha Stenge, winner of most of the national quilt contests in the 20th century, made the "Bible Quilt" after it was featured in *Ladies' Home Journal*. Instead of the suggested cottons, she chose satin. The quilt won a prize at the 1949 Tennessee State Fair and was included in the 1950 Mountain Mist Blue Book of State Fair winners. When Bertha died in 1957, her quilts were either distributed to family members or sold. The whereabouts of her "Bible Quilt" is unknown. (For more information about Bertha, see *page 67*.)

Although Nancy Oakley wrote about the popularity of quilts in her June 1931 "The Hostess" column and included a floral appliqué quilt, she seemed more awed by quilts than filled with desire to make one.

"For those of you who have June brides in your immediate circle, you will surely want at least one or two notes that have the dignity of old, established custom to recommend them.

"Certainly, quilts for the bride's room, or for the gay new guest room, fit this requirement in a specially satisfying fashion. They seem to belong to old mahogany and the traditions of beautiful stately homes in the country, surrounded by old-fashioned, fragrant gardens such as our grandmothers loved.

"But they are very much the fad of the moment too. They will fit in the tiniest, gayest, two-rooms-and-kitchenette apartment. Or in a seashore bungalow. Or in an English Early Colonial house in the suburbs. So I am showing you what I think is a very delightful old-new quilt on our Hostess page this month.

"As yet, I haven't heard of quilting bees coming back in popularity; but if the present quilting craze keeps up long enough, who can say whether we shan't revive them, too, in the wake of a dozen other old customs. And wouldn't that be amusing."

In the April 1933 *Ladies' Home Journal*, the editors promoted four patterns using the familiar Colonial Revival/quilt revival themes. "Make an heirloom, it's new and easy-to-make," readers were encouraged. The "Cherry Ripe" quilt featured a cheery block with four clusters of 15 cherries, green leaves, and stems to appliqué. "Star Diamond" was a complex pieced pattern. (To make this quilt, see *page 104*.) "Wild Rose" was a simplified version of a Marie Webster appliqué pattern offered through the magazine several years earlier. And "Colonial Dame" featured a Colonial silhouette of a young woman in a bonnet carrying a nosegay in her hand. This block was designed to alternate with gingham blocks. Readers could purchase the patterns for 10 cents each.

Though Ladies' Home Journal published far fewer patterns, the magazine still promoted quilts as essential for home decorating.

SURVEY SAYS: QUILTS ARE HOT STUFF

In 1934, the Stearns & Foster Co. published an advertising guide, "The Romance of Quilt making Sales," for department stores carrying the company's quilt patterns and products. Until the end of the 1920s, most quilters lived on farms or in small towns, according to company research. But the market was changing. The booklet reported:

"Recent surveys show that at least 400 metropolitan newspapers are publishing quilt material regularly. A Gallup survey in six large cities shows further that the quilt article is the most popular Sunday feature—32% of the women reading it. Many of these newspapers have sponsored quilt shows and had attendances numbering into the tens of thousands."

The Stearns & Foster Co. announced their campaign to advertise in "six magazines with a total circulation of 9,845,938 or two out of every five women in the country." *Better Homes and Gardens* and *Ladies' Home Journal* were included in the group of six.

OLD-FASHIONED NOSEGAY is also known as BRIDE'S BOUQUET. c. 1940; 83½×98"

> ❝❝ Is your eightsome playing bridge every meeting? Lots of them aren't because quilts are crowding contract, and in many smart communities it looks as if the Q's have it!"
>
> —Emma Tyrrell, *Better Homes and Gardens*, February 1932

ANTIQUE QUILTS INSPIRE EMMA TYRRELL

In the January 1931 *Better Homes and Gardens* article entitled "Quilts of Great-Grandmother's Day—Brought to You in These Authentic Copies," Emma Tyrrell shared her first attempt as a 6-year-old at making a four-patch quilt under the guidance of her mother. She also discussed her hobby of collecting authentic old quilt patterns; six were featured in this article.

She shared an enchanting and touching quilt story, whether true or not, that added to the mystique of quiltmaking in the 1930s:

"A Pennsylvania family was fording a river in Iowa when their trunk containing books and a precious Oak Leaf and Acorn quilt became dislodged from the wagon and floated quickly downstream. The following winter, while staying at a farm not far from the river, they talked of their journey and yearned for the lost quilt. The women of the family reproduced the quilt from memory. The next spring they returned to Pennsylvania.

"One day the woman who had sheltered the Pennsylvanians went to visit a friend who lived farther south, some 25 miles by wagon road. And there, on her friend's best bed, she saw the Oak Leaf and Acorn quilt like the one her visitor had talked about. Moreover, in the corner were the initials and the date, 1831."

For a February 1933 quilt article, Emma returned to old quilt patterns and antique quilts for inspiration. She wrote, "Quilts may come and quilts may go, but still the quilt designs that Grandmother found suitable for her household are among our loveliest and most popular designs today. You have but to go to a quilt fair to find this out yourself." She featured old pieced "Log Cabin" patterns and "Devil's Claw." For appliqué, she included photographs of antique quilts from Kentucky and Ohio with the names "Ohio Rose," "Rose of Sharon," and "Democratic Rose."

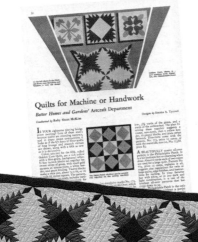

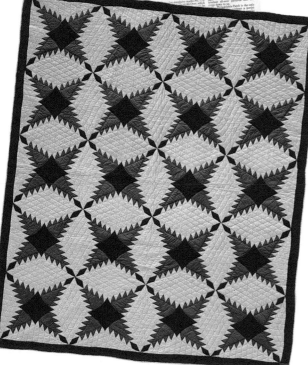

Sometimes known as PINE BURR, this quilt is similar to the pattern Emma Tyrrell called THE PHILADELPHIA PATCH. c. 1900; 73×90"

MYSTERY WRITER

Late in 1933, Ruby Short McKim's name mysteriously disappeared from the pages of *Better Homes and Gardens*, replaced by Doris Hale. Quilt researcher Jill Sutton Filo began to suspect that Doris Hale might be Ruby after discovering that a few McKim patterns were offered in the November 1933 issue through the Artcraft Department "conducted by Doris Hale."

Historian Susan Miller examined a letter signed by Doris Hale and sent to Iowa quiltmaker Lillian Walker on November 26, 1935. Although the letter was written on stationery with a letterhead *Better Homes and Gardens*, Des Moines, Iowa, the postmark city on the envelope was Independence, Missouri, home of McKim Studios.

Why Ruby's byline would change to Doris Hale is unclear. The mystery becomes even murkier when one examines the November 1935 article "Quilts with Ancient Heritage," shown *below*, signed by Doris Hale. Both the style and content pertaining to old quilt pattern names and vintage quilts reflected Emma Tyrrell's columns, while the pattern "Fan Star" resembles the colorful quilts designed by Hubert Ver Mehren. Nevertheless, the three patterns appeared in McKim advertising in the 1930s. There is little doubt that Ruby McKim was the originator. We may never know if Doris Hale actually existed.

FAN STAR appeared in the November 1935 Better Homes and Gardens *article by Doris Hale. c. 1935; 79×85"*

Did Ruby McKim's work appear in 1930s issues of Better Homes and Gardens as Doris Hale's? It's a mystery.

RUBY SHORT McKIM'S QUILT KITS

Since its inception in the late 1920s, McKim Studios sold packaged kits of supplies for an array of crafts and needlework projects, including some pieced and appliqué quilts. Beginning in 1930, Ruby also offered pieced quilts "ready-cut for easy pick-up work." It wasn't until the November 1935 issue that she first sold patterns for center-medallion appliqué quilts. In this *Better Homes and Gardens* article, *right*, written by Doris Hale, three quilts are featured. The two ready-cut pieced quilts— "Fan Star," shown *above right*, and "Snail's Trail"—were offered in gold, rose, or blue. Each was sold with the pattern only for 15 cents or as ready-cut pieces with accompanying pattern for $5.00. The "First Lady" appliqué quilt kit came with stamped materials and instruction sheet. There was no pattern provided because, as Doris explained in a letter to inquiring quiltmaker Lillian Walker: "We do not ordinarily furnish the patterns to the First Lady quilt because they are large by the time you count the wreath, bolster, scallop, bow and all the other appliqués. However, we will make an exception in your case and furnish these stamped from our Master Pattern onto paper so you can copy them. [The cost is] 75 cents for the complete set and the instruction chart."

The Medallion Man
Hubert Ver Mehren

Although the name Hubert Ver Mehren never appeared in *Successful Farming*, the quilt patterns and products of this Des Moines businessman did illustrate several articles in the magazine during the 1930s.

Hubert produced stamped quilt blocks for embroidery, stamped fabric for quilt kits, quilt patterns, quilting designs, and colorful catalogs at his Iowa Button and Pleating Company. In 1932, he published the booklet "Colonial Quilts," shown *above right*, featuring "old and new" quilt designs. *Successful Farming* offered the booklet for 25 cents, calling it "*Successful Farming's* Colonial Quilt Book." Other magazines and newspapers sold the identical booklet as a service of their own quilt column editors.

Hubert Ver Mehren's quilt patterns were best-sellers in the pages of Successful Farming, but quilters had no idea that he was the designer.

Hubert had moved from Omaha after World War I to establish a Des Moines branch of his father's button and pleating business. In the mid-1920s, he began stamping quilt blocks, pillowcases, and linens with matching designs for embroidery in a variety of colorful threads that became available. For the most part, he adapted motifs and themes already on the market for these popular printed goods, though around 1930 he started selling traditional pieced quilt patterns.

When his arrangement of four shades of one color for a "Lone Star" quilt caught the attention of quiltmakers, he created other, more original medallion designs with elegant and complex quilting that greatly enhanced the total effect.

While Hubert's wife, Mary, was at home caring for the couple's two children, she operated a retail mail-order business called Home Art Studios that sold Iowa Button and Pleating products as well as items from other sources. Eventually, Hubert added the Home Art Studios name to his quilt patterns, the only label that has identified them. He kept his name away from public attention since his primary job was to provide products for other businesses to sell.

Though yellow was the favorite color of quilters who ordered Hubert's medallion kits, they were also available in pink, blue, and orchid.
GOLDEN DAHLIA, c. 1934; 81" square

His center medallion quilt kits were offered in his catalog in "four harmonizing shades of the following colors—pink, blue, orchid, and yellow." These quilts today are Hubert's signature designs. Introduced in 1932, they quickly gained popularity among quiltmakers entering the 1933 Sears Roebuck & Co. National Quilt Contest. Two of Hubert's quilts reached the final round of thirty: "Star of France" by Susie Combs of Kentucky, and "Rising Sun" by Lillie Belle Carpenter of Pennsylvania.

Hubert's bold center medallion designs, displayed vertically, thrilled not only the judges, but also quilt show visitors. Visually, they outshone the sweet floral pastel appliqués; technically, the piecing and quilting required a high level of sewing skills.

In November 1932, *Successful Farming*, shown *right*, offered Hubert's "May Day Flower Basket" quilt as a set of 32 embroidered designs, each with different flowers. The baskets came stamped on white muslin, sateen, or broadcloth. The package cost $1 to $1.75 based on the fabric chosen. Readers could also order "*Successful Farming*'s Colonial Quilt Book."

In March 1933, another of Hubert's embroidered quilts called "Blossom Time" was sold as a set of 32 cloth blocks with stamped designs of lilac, goldenrod, June rose, geranium, cornflower, pond lily, and California poppy for $1. In June 1933, as regular readers of *Successful Farming* opened their magazines, they might have been surprised to find a quilt article inside the front cover—in color, no less. Titled "New and Old Quilts," the article shown *far right* featured a reproduction of an Early American quilt the author, Lou Ann Rogers, had seen in Kentucky the previous summer. Called "Constellation," the quilt was made of two distinct blocks—a pieced block called Feathered Star and an appliqué block of circles called A Planet Field. Unbleached muslin was suggested

In addition to his coveted quilt kits, Hubert sold stamped fabric for embroidering quilt blocks. His "May Day Flower Basket" quilt included 32 blocks.

for the background and colored print cottons for the pieces. The pattern and quilting design cost 10 cents. The new design was called "Rose Arbor," a design in Hubert Ver Mehren's 1932 "Colonial Quilts" booklet. As with all of Hubert's patterns, a specific quilting design was recommended for each quilt. The perforated quilting design cost an additional 10 cents.

Hubert's kits for his medallion quilts included fabric stamped with cutting and sewing lines for each geometric piece.

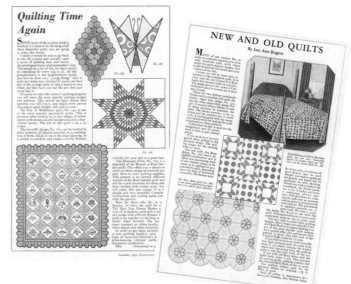

Above: *The November 1932 issue of* Successful Farming *featured Hubert's "Lone Star" quilt.*

After the 1940s, as interest in quilting waned, quilting stories in Better Homes and Gardens *and* Successful Farming *grew sporadic. Instead, menu planning and cooking features became more prominent as the* Better Homes and Gardens *Test Kitchen gained recognition.*

1940-1969
The Middle Years

Armed with the slogan "Never Underestimate the Power of a Woman," Ladies' Home Journal reached more than 4.5 million readers in the early 1950s.

AS EARLY AS WORLD WAR II, THE TIMES, THEY WERE A-CHANGING, AS THE '60S SONG WOULD LATER SAY. WHILE THEIR HUSBANDS FOUGHT ABROAD, WOMEN LEFT HOME TO WORK BUT CONTINUED TO QUILT. FOR THE NEXT 25 YEARS, AS SYNTHETIC FABRICS FLOURISHED AND ANYTHING OLD BECAME UNFASHIONABLE, IT WAS UP TO DEDICATED CRAFTERS TO KEEP QUILTING TRADITIONS ALIVE.

Embroidered and appliquéd quilts designed by Marion Cheever Whiteside (see profile, page 68) with fairy tale and fictional characters were popular with quilters in the 1950s.
LITTLE WOMEN, c. 1950; 88×103"

Finally believing that the hard times of the Great Depression were over, Americans awoke with a jolt on December 7, 1941, to the Japanese bombing of Pearl Harbor. Strict rationing of food and materials as well as the draft of tens of thousands of young men thrust the war into the lives of American families.

For four years, the nation summoned its resources, made sacrifices, and worked toward the common goal of winning the war.

The postwar boom period found many women living in spanking-new suburban homes and raising a brood of children. Parenting, meal planning, and interior decorating occupied their daily lives, while television provided nightly entertainment for the whole family. By the late 1950s, most Americans had experienced a decade of prosperity that was unequaled in the nation's history. The Korean War was over, and although the Cold War had begun, Americans were enjoying their status as citizens of the world's first "superpower."

The election of the youthful John F. Kennedy as president in 1960 began an even more hopeful era. Popular causes, such as the Civil Rights movement, equal rights for women, and the environmental movement, swept the country as people protested against long-standing injustices. The space program was played out on television sets nationwide, and Americans could watch the miraculous events that culminated in the first moon walk. But the Cuban missile crisis, Vietnam War, antiwar demonstrations, and a string of assassinations cast a pall over this time period.

A Revolution in Fabrics

The three wars in which the United States participated between 1940 and 1969 often affected fabric design, usage, and availability. World War II cut deeply into domestic textile

In the 1950s with the population booming, novelty or "conversation prints" that depicted make-believe and cartoon characters appealed to families with young children.

The Middle Years

1941 December 7: Japan attacks the United States naval base at Pearl Harbor and the U.S. enters World War II; *Better Homes and Gardens* publishes the first national barbecue story. **1943** The Jitterbug is the popular dance. **1944** June 6: The Allies invade Europe on D-Day. **1945** World War II ends; *Better Homes and Gardens* introduces the family room. **1949** The Pillsbury Bake-Off

58   Century *of* Quilts

production but also led to a rising patriotism; red, white, and blue designs featuring stars, military insignia, nautical images, and Uncle Sam top hats appeared on both domestic and feed-sack cottons. As women went to war and to work outside their homes, they often wore job-related uniforms rather than dresses, reducing their sewing needs. Home sewing was directed toward remaking earlier garments in updated styles, rather than the construction of clothing from whatever new fabrics might be available.

The postwar fabric design and goods suggest a "baby boom" preoccupation with home and family. Popular were children's prints featuring Disney characters, cowboys, and baby animals. Cottons for home use often carried designs such as fruit, life-size flowers, kitchen implements, and garden tools. Strong colors were terra-cotta

During World War II, fabric designs reflected the patriotic spirit of home sewers.

begins as the Great National Recipe and Baking Contest.

1950 North Korea invades South Korea; Frank X. McNamara introduces Diner's Club, the first credit card; and cartoonist Charles Schulz's comic strip *Peanuts* debuts in seven newspapers.

1951 Color television has first telecast. **1952** Coronation of Elizabeth II takes place. **1953** Sir Edmund Hillary reaches the summit of Mount Everest.

and moss green, often used with soft butter yellow. And although they might sew for family and home, a generation of nonquilters emerged who preferred to buy premade rather than create homemade bedding in the prosperous postwar years.

As women turned away from quiltmaking, the market for cotton fabrics declined. In the 1940s and 1950s "miracle" fabrics for home sewing appeared. Synthetics, such as nylon, rayon, acetate, Celanese, and Dacron, and fabrics with permanent pleats or crease-resistant finishes promised relief from the drudgery of ironing. Some companies continued to offer the old standards in calicoes: little flowers in double pink, medium blue, green, yellow, or lavender with yellow centers. For a time in the 1950s and 1960s, these were the only colors and designs available in cotton fabrics for quilters.

The launching of Sputnik in 1957 inspired fabrics printed with rockets, ringed moons, and satellites. The favored colors at different times during the 1950s were lime green or chartreuse, aqua, pink, and brown.

The earth tones of the 1960s were often overshadowed by fabrics in lime green, hot pink, and aqua.

In the early 1960s, the back-to-nature movement led to widespread interest in natural foods, simpler lifestyles, and home sewing and quiltmaking. Preferred fabric colors were earth tones in rust, copper, beige, dark gold, olive green, and similar shades. During the Vietnam War, counterculture movements were associated with fabrics in hot, psychedelic colors and oversize floral motifs (remember "flower power"?), as well as fabrics printed with peace signs and other pacifist images.

Late in the period, the public embraced polyester double-knit fabric, which was washable, pliable, wrinkle-free, and virtually indestructible. Many Amish women quickly adopted double-knit for its versatility in garment construction and quiltmaking. Despite the material's weight and thickness, the women used it to fashion such solid-color designs as "Giant Dahlia" and "Grandmother's Flower Garden," making colorful and durable quilts.

Fabrics made from synthetic fibers were great for easy-care garments, but not at all desirable for crafting quilts.

The Middle Years

1953 The Korean War ends.   **1954** Jonas Salk creates the polio vaccine.

1955 Ray Kroc opens the first McDonald's restaurant; Disneyland opens.

1957 *American Bandstand* debuts on national television with host Dick Clark.

1959 Alaska and Hawaii become the 49th and 50th states.

1962 John Glenn is first American to orbit the Earth.

1963 November 22: President John F. Kennedy is assassinated in Dallas.

Bright saturated colors remained popular in quilts of the 1950s and 1960s.
FLOWERPOTS, c. 1950; 72×80"

1963 Betty Friedan writes *The Feminine Mystique*, galvanizing the new feminist movement. **1964** The Civil Rights Act passes. **1965** The United States enters the Vietnam conflict; the St. Louis Gateway Arch, designed by Eero Saarinen, is completed; the first countertop microwave oven for the home is produced by Amana. **1967** Dr. Christiaan Barnard performs the first heart transplant. **1969** Neil Armstrong becomes the first man to walk on the moon's surface.

DRESDEN PLATE, popular during the 1930s, continued to be a favorite with quilters throughout the next decade as the article, right, *from the February 1941 issue of* Successful Farming *suggests. c. 1935; 79×96¼"*

MAGAZINES ON A ROLL IN THE 1940S

Aunt Martha quilt and needlework patterns published in Kansas City by the Colonial Quilt Company composed a syndicated line that began appearing in *Successful Farming* in the late 1930s. The quilt patterns were often combined with other needlework projects, as in the October 1940 *Successful Farming* article titled "New for Gifts and Bazaars." The article's illustrations for patterns for two quilts share the page with stuffed dolls, pot holders, an apron, and kitchen linens. In other articles, only one quilt pattern is featured with the ordering information.

The February 1941 *Successful Farming, opposite,* carried a full page of Aunt Martha quilts, extolling them as "quilts of today's making become tomorrow's treasures, gaining in loveliness and sentiment with each passing year." All were well-known patterns ("Dresden Plate," "Friendship Dahlia," "Sunflower," and "Grandmother's Flower Garden") except the "Flower Basket" made of 12 baskets with a different appliqué bloom for each block.

In April 1943, *Successful Farming* again featured four patterns, *right.* An "American Beauty" appliqué must have reminded readers

of mid-1800s "Rose of Sharon" appliqué designs. The other three were pieced patterns: an easy one called "Double Tulip"; the "Aunt Martha Rose," which combined print calicoes set against plain green and white diamonds; and the 15-inch block called "Geometric Puzzle" that appears in the upper left corner of the page. With its 89 pieces, it would be a challenge for a beginner. (To make a quilt based on this pattern, see *page 112*.)

Many of the quilting patterns offered for sale by magazines in the 1940s were classic quilt designs.

THOROUGHLY MODERN QUILTING

In Christine Ferry's April 1940 article "To Quilt Is Smartly Modern," in *Better Homes and Gardens*, she recommended letting the sewing machine speed the job: "Although to Grandma, something quilted meant something nice and warm to snuggle under in bed … today its handsome texture is big news in other fields. Clothes, draperies, upholstery, and slip-covers claim it, and amateurs and experts all over the place are relearning the simple old art of quilting.

"You CAN have your quilting done, but loads of women are doing it themselves, either by hand or on the sewing machine. A special presser-foot attachment regulates spaces between diagonal lines of a plaided [sic] background. If you work by hand, mark guide lines lightly with pencil and yardstick."

In the 1940s, *Ladies' Home Journal* was still selling four patterns from the previous decade: "Bible Quilt," "Cherry Ripe Quilt," "Star Diamond Quilt," and "Wild Rose."

In November 1940, the magazine added three new quilt patterns designed by Bertha Stenge. (For more information about Bertha, see *page 67*.) All three patterns featured stuffed appliqué as well as trapunto and cording: "Iva's Pin Cushion," "Ruth's Ring," and "Rachel's Wreath." These were difficult projects requiring a high skill level in both quilting and appliqué.

In 1941, *Ladies' Home Journal* introduced quilt kits to its readers. Interior Decoration Editor Henrietta Murdock wrote, "Most of us are unaware that department stores now have complete quilt kits from about $3.29 to $6.98. It's easy to cut out all the little appliqué shapes, too, for they are all stamped on colored bits of material, ready for your scissors. And these gaily colored spreads with their light backgrounds never cost you any cleaner's bills, either, for all the materials are guaranteed tubfast." Sadly, a year later due to cloth shortages related to the war, such quilt kits were hard to find.

Judy Reece's JACK-IN-THE-BEANSTALK, c. 1941

Before the cloth shortages during World War II, quilters could easily buy kits for patterns such as "Jack-in-the-Beanstalk."

This April 1941 article, *left*, featured kits that came with white percale quilt tops stamped for appliqué, as well as a quilt lining marked for quilting designs. The patterns were "Wild Rose," "Sunflower," and a crib-size quilt featuring the fairy-tale characters from Jack and the Beanstalk, shown *above*.

For the January 1943 issue of *Ladies' Home Journal*, Henrietta Murdock came up with some home-front ideas to "help you pass the time and you'll treasure them in years to come. A war baby's rug embroidered 'Vitamins for Victory.' A welcome home hooked rug—with a U. S. eagle. A child's place mat, 'Clean Up Your Plate for Victory.'"

Henrietta also suggested military wives form quilt clubs. Each member would appliqué her husband's service insignia on a square, join the blocks together, and quilt it up. "Make one quilt each," she wrote.

Anne Orr (see profile, *page 66*) opens with a subtle reference to the limitations of the war years in her 1943 two-part article "Quilt Today for the Warmth, the Fun, and the Beauty of It," in *Better Homes and Gardens*: "We're quiltmaking again—and we love it! Maybe those hard-to-come-by items—fuel and wool—have inspired us. Or maybe it's just that we've discovered all over what our pioneer great-grandmothers knew all the time—that working a quilt is the most fascinating of handcrafts, and a beautiful quilt made by your own hands is a treasure for today and tomorrow."

An April 1944 *Ladies' Home Journal* article, *above*, featured a "Victory Quilt" made in just two months by Virginia T. Osborne: "This is the way the quilt is made: Twelve white blocks with blue fields appliquéd on, white stars on the blue, and appliquéd red strips—all combining patriotically to combine it with the music—God Bless America—to your linen closet!" The pattern was offered for just 10 cents.

ORIGINAL QUILTS GRACE SUCCESSFUL FARMING

In 1952, *Successful Farming* included a quilt article, shown *opposite*, featuring two well-known quiltmakers, Bertha Stenge (see profile, *page 67*) and Florence Peto. One of the featured quilts, the "Strawberry Royal Quilt," was an antique from Florence's collection, described as "traditional, yet simple enough to go with most modern furniture." The "Barbara Rose Quilt" designed and made by Bertha Stenge was described as "also lending itself smartly to today's room settings." Both quilt designs were sold through *Successful Farming* for the cost of "6 cents each to cover mailing costs."

One wonders if Bertha and Florence might have been surprised (even a little appalled) at the interior decorator's suggestions for taking one quilt motif and using it painted on a cabinet door panel, stenciled on a wall alcove, and appliquéd on bolsters and pillows. The article ended with a cautionary word: "Unless an actual room is very large, one should guard against using too many repeats in a single room."

The only quilt article, shown *left,* in the 1960s in *Successful Farming* was one marking the centennial of the start of the American Civil War. "A Quilt Spans a Century" featured a quilt owned by Clara Landis Pinther of Columbus, Ohio. The feature reported: "In 1860, Mrs. Lucinda Dugan of Delaware, Ohio, completed two identical quilts in an original design, which she called 'Queen's Feathers.' She gave each of her two sons one of these quilts upon his return from the Civil War. Today, only one of these quilts remains."

Along with the family's story of "Queen's Feathers," the *Successful Farming* decorators placed the 100-year-old quilt in a "Country Traditional" room to prove its versatility, claiming "it is just as much at home with today's decorating trends as it was in its own day. Make a copy of this handsome quilt. Choose colors for the quilt that blend with the existing colors of the room, or create an exciting new color scheme with your heirloom quilt as the starting point."

TRAILBLAZING DESIGN OF THE '60S

In the 1960s, *Better Homes and Gardens* offered many contemporary designs in bold, solid colors of the day—chartreuse, lavender, aquamarine, yellow, and orange—often in simplified appliqué shapes such as large-petaled, stylized flowers and birds.

Of the credited designers published in *Better Homes and Gardens*, Jean Ray Laury became one of the best known. Her quilt career began when she entered a contest in 1958. Although she did not win a prize for her quilt, she caught the attention of one of the judges, an editor for *House Beautiful,* who invited her to write an article for the magazine's January 1960 issue.

Jean soon received requests to do classes and lectures. She is credited as one of the first contemporary quilting teachers who encouraged beginners to reinvent quiltmaking for themselves by experimenting with old techniques and new ideas. She wrote one of the first contemporary quilting books, *Appliqué Stitchery* (1966), and *Quilts & Coverlets: A Contemporary Approach* (1970), which brought her to the attention of *Better Homes and Gardens.* (To make a pillow inspired by a Jean Ray Laury design, see *page 117.*)

Traditional-style quilts, left, continued to appeal to magazine readers through the '50s. With the dawning of the '60s, quilt design was destined to go in a new direction.

Meredith's Quilting Stars
Anne Orr

During the 1940s, *Better Homes and Gardens* greatly reduced its quilt pattern articles. In the previous decade the magazine had attained a certain status as the place to turn to for quilt patterns, even though the patterns were sold through the McKim Studios in Independence, Missouri. Although quilting articles were not featured in the magazine as often, *Better Homes and Gardens* did reach out to well-known needlework designer Anne Orr.

A Nashville socialite and newlywed in 1894, Anne was selected as art editor in 1913 for *Southern Woman*, a magazine published by several prominent local women. Anne wrote a monthly column reflecting her interests in collecting antiques, crocheting, cross-stitch, embroidery, knitting, needlepoint, and tatting.

Two years later, she began selling needlepoint designs by mail and would later become needlework editor at *Good Housekeeping* for 20 years. She copyrighted the patterns and sold them through the magazine as well as through her own studio. In the 1930s with quilting at the peak of popularity, Anne shifted gears and added quilts and quilt patterns to her business, The Anne Orr Studio.

Eventually recognized as a fine quilt designer, Anne was selected to be a judge at one of the prestigious Eastern States Exposition quilt contests in 1932 and for the Sears Roebuck & Co. National Quilt Contest in 1933. She also published two quilting books, *Set 100 Quilts and Quilting* (1932) and *Anne Orr Quilts* (1944). Anne Orr-designed quilts in the *Better*

Originally a needlework designer, Anne Orr adapted her designs for quilting.

Some of Anne's appliqué designs, such as MAY BASKET, above, and POPPY, left, were reminiscent of the 1910 designs of Marie Webster.

Homes and Gardens articles were not specifically mentioned in the magazine's ordering instructions.

Above: Made of 1-inch squares, Anne Orr's FRENCH WREATH quilt is based on a cross-stitch pattern.

Meredith's Quilting Stars
Bertha Stenge

In the mid 1940s, the *Chicago Tribune* proclaimed designer Bertha Stenge "An Artist with a Needle" and "Chicago's Quilting Queen." *Woman's Day* called her designs "the cream of the nation's needle crop." A *Newsweek* art critic pronounced her quilts "the finest modern quilts in the United States today."

Born in 1891, Bertha attended the San Francisco School of Art and learned to design stained-glass windows. In 1929, while confined to her bed recovering from an illness, Bertha made her first quilt: a Nancy Page "Grandmother's Garden" series quilt that she

entered in a contest sponsored by the *Chicago Evening American*. Bertha's quilt won a $25 second-place prize.

She later entered the 1933 Sears Roebuck & Co. National Quilt Contest at the Chicago World's Fair with a quilt of her own design depicting 100 years of Chicago's history. However, the judges overlooked the pictorial quilts and awarded the $1,000 grand prize to a traditional quilt featuring trapunto quilting.

For her next contest, Bertha made a "Palm Leaf" quilt with elaborate trapunto quilting and won first place in a local contest. That quilt also earned her more than $700 prize money in the 1940 New York World's Fair contest.

Confident that sophisticated and innovative techniques combined with traditional quilt patterns would mean more prizes from contest judges, Bertha produced several more quilts with original trapunto designs: "Rachel's Wreath" (1935), "Iva's Pin Cushion" (1936), and "Ruth's Ring" (1937).

Quilts Bertha made in 1943 and 1950 were selected among the top 100 quilts of the 20th century.

Illustrations of these three quilts, which were described as "modern-looking," appeared in the November 1940 issue of *Ladies' Home Journal.* For 10 cents, readers could buy the pattern to make a quilt designed by Bertha Stenge.

In the 1942 Woman's Day National Needlework Exhibition, her quilts took several

Above: *IVA'S PIN CUSHION was based on a microscopic image of a snowflake. Bertha's incredible trapunto work is featured in RACHEL'S WREATH, top right, and RUTH'S RING, bottom right.*

prizes. Her "Victory" quilt not only won the $100 prize in the appliqué division, but also the $1,000 grand prize for best of show. Her other entry titled "Peace" won a third-place $25 award in the quilting category. Asked how she'd spend the prize money, Bertha said she'd buy war bonds.

The wire services sent Bertha's photograph and story to newsrooms throughout the country. Her life story made for interesting copy. She was a mother, a Red Cross volunteer, and an artist. Bertha continued to make quilts. Her designs were featured again in *Ladies' Home Journal* in 1947.

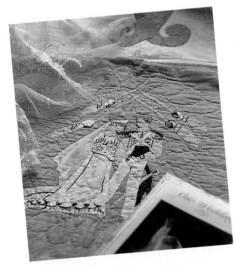

BRIDAL QUILT, based on international bridal customs, was Marion's first quilt published in Ladies' Home Journal. *c. 1949; 84×97"*

Meredith's Quilting Stars
Marion Cheever Whiteside

Nine pictorial appliqué quilts designed by Marion Cheever Whiteside were published in *Ladies' Home Journal* between 1949 and 1961. Marion, who studied art in New York City and Paris, opened Story Book Quilts in 1940, selling ready-made and custom-made quilts. It is estimated that she designed more than 50 appliqué patterns and produced more than 3,000 quilts from 1940 to 1960.

Her first quilt was the "Bible Quilt," based on a design she probably saw in *Ladies' Home Journal* in August 1938 (see *page 49*). She reworked some scenes and added others to make the quilt for her nephew George, who remembered the bedtime stories each block evoked. Marion soon received requests for this quilt, and a cottage industry was born. She employed some seamstresses to sew the appliqué blocks and others to stitch blocks and quilt the layers together.

During the 1940s, Marion was invited to exhibit "Story Book Quilts" in New York, New Jersey, and Michigan. In 1945, the Metropolitan Museum of Art commissioned her to make an "Alice in Wonderland Quilt." She was also asked to design the "History of Baseball" quilt for the Baseball Museum in Cooperstown, New York.

Ladies' Home Journal featured the following patterns by Marion: "Bridal Quilt" (February 1949); "Circus Quilt" and a 15-block "Little Women" (October 1950), which became one of her most familiar designs; "Lucky Day" and "Baby Animals" (March 1954); "State Flower" (February 1955); "Peter Pan" (December 1956); "Pinocchio" (January 1958); and "Firemen" (November 1961).

Marion's quilts alternated picture blocks with plain blocks. Her patterns contained full-size line drawings of the appliqué scene, from which the quiltmaker had to cut her own templates. A black-and-white photograph of the completed quilt was on the front of the pattern envelope. Each pattern cost 25 cents.

Marion's quilts were not artistic masterpieces, but children loved them.

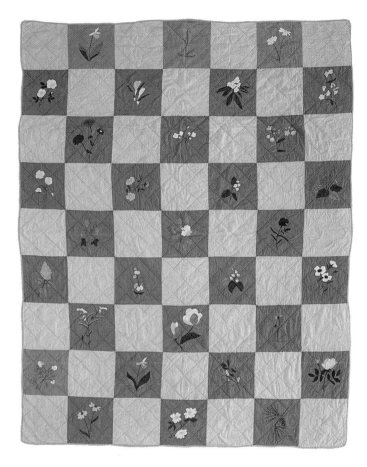

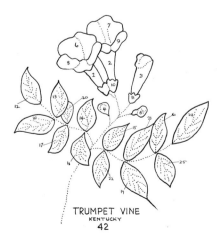

TRUMPET VINE
KENTUCKY
42

Left *and* above: *Sample block patterns from Marion's* STATE FLOWER QUILT, top, *featured in* Ladies' Home Journal *in 1955.*

The foundation of Meredith's publishing venture for years was its first two magazines, Successful Farming *and* Better Homes and Gardens. *In 1986,* Ladies' Home Journal *became part of the publishing family. Later, Meredith would add brand-new magazines to the list—*Midwest Living, Country Home, Traditional Home, *and* More*—as well as books and hundreds of newsstand magazines created especially for crafting, decorating, cooking, gardening, building, remodeling, and quilting.*

1970-2002

A Quilting Revival

With its launch in 1993, American Patchwork & Quilting *magazine became a reliable resource for patterns and techniques for quilters.*

WITH ITS 200TH BIRTHDAY IN 1976, AMERICA TOOK A LOOK BACK WITH NEW APPRECIATION FOR QUILTING. CRAFTERS TURNED TO BETTER HOMES AND GARDENS AS A SOURCE FOR BOTH TRADITIONAL AND CONTEMPORARY DESIGNS. AS INTEREST IN THE CRAFT CONTINUED TO GROW, MEREDITH CORPORATION CREATED A BIMONTHLY MAGAZINE JUST FOR QUILTERS: AMERICAN PATCHWORK & QUILTING.

RAILROAD CROSSING, which appeared in American Patchwork & Quilting *magazine, was designed by Cindy Blackberg. Like many contemporary quilters, she likes to reproduce classic quilt designs using new color combinations and modern piecing techniques. c. 1999; 52×66"*

Remembered as a somewhat turbulent time in the nation's history, the 1970s was a transitional era. Caught between the postwar optimism of the 1950s and idealism of the 1960s, and the coming boom years of the 1980s, America was finding its way in the 1970s. The decade is now known for its continued political and social protests, an oil embargo, government scandals, energy and hostage crises, and the rise of the "Me Generation."

By the early 1980s, Americans were caught up in the pursuit of money and status. The next decade brought personal computers, VCRs, video games, electronic organizers, cellular phones, and pagers into the homes of most Americans. By the end of the 1990s, the world had become a giant community connected by the World Wide Web.

A MUSEUM SHOW AND THE BICENTENNIAL REVIVE QUILTING

In 1971, the Whitney Museum of American Art sponsored an exhibit called "Abstract Design in American Quilts." Superb geometric Amish quilts and even mundane scrap quilts impressed

In the 1970s, women found fulfillment in designing, drafting, and making original quilts.

viewers with their artistic qualities. The media coverage and subsequent touring shows raised public awareness of quilts.

With the approach of the 200th anniversary of the signing of the Declaration of Independence in 1976, interest in making quilts increased. Individuals, quilting clubs and classes, community groups, and schoolchildren participated by creating commemorative quilts. Magazines and newspapers offered patterns and kits, sponsored contests, and featured stories about historic quilts and quiltmakers.

By the time the Bicentennial arrived, quilters had made great strides in learning what was almost a lost art. Designers and crafters used trial and error to figure out how to put fabric and batting together, developing new techniques, and expanding the domain of quilts greatly. Their efforts, along with the national interest in the Bicentennial, exposed quilting to an ever-growing audience of creative individuals who were eager to learn the craft of their grandmothers.

NEW OLD-STYLE FABRICS

As the second major quilt revival of the 20th century gained momentum, the textile industry slowly began to answer the need for appropriate fabrics. Focus on the Bicentennial directed public attention to the quilts that were a part of America's heritage. Red, white, and blue fabrics, some with eagles, stars, and other Bicentennial designs, rose in popularity, as did decorator

A Quilting Revival

1971 Intel introduces the microprocessor; Starbucks Coffee opens its first location at Seattle's Pike Place Market. **1972** M*A*S*H, the popular television series based on a mobile surgical unit during the Korean War, begins an 11-season run. **1974** Richard Nixon resigns as President. **1976** The United States celebrates its Bicentennial. **1979** OLFA develops the first rotary cutter; the first International Quilt Market—the only trade show for the quilting

1776–1976

As quilting made a comeback, quilters had more options than ever for combining colors and fabrics to create new designs for such projects as this 1985 patchwork duvet, which could be adjusted to fit any bed size.

industry—is held in Houston, Texas. **1980** The American Quilt Study Group (AQSG) is founded. **1981** IBM introduces the personal computer; Sandra Day O'Connor becomes the first woman Supreme Court justice.

1982 The blockbuster movie *E.T.: The Extraterrestrial* opens in theaters.

1985 The American Quilter's Society (AQS), founded a year earlier to recognize quilting as an art form, holds its first quilt show and contest in Paducah, Kentucky.

AMERICAN
QUILTER'S
SOCIETY
Quilt Show
APRIL 26-28, 1985

A
Q S

Paducah, Kentucky
SHOW BOOKLET

Cotton fabrics made a comeback in the '70s, thanks to quilters' demands. Bright colors and abstract designs coexisted with fabric created especially for the Bicentennial in 1976.

fabrics with Colonial and Early American images. It wasn't long before fabric manufacturers began to look at early textiles and how they might be reproduced.

Jinny Beyer has been influential in designing modern textiles, especially fabrics that echo the look of 19th-century goods. She may have been the first designer to have her imprint on the selvage, although others had signature lines through their own companies. Following Jinny's lead, designers ventured into the market, beginning tentatively with "sea foam" double-pink reproductions and gradually encompassing most of the major fabric looks, colors, and combinations of the past 200 years. These designers have vied for new groupings to reproduce, scouring antique markets, antique quilts, and other sources for early fabric samples on which to base new lines.

Another influential designer, Jean Ray Laury, introduced a contemporary approach to quiltmaking, and the art quilt was born. After reading her book *Quilts and Coverlets: A Contemporary Approach* published in 1970, quilters began asking for fabrics in bold, innovative designs and colors, and fabric manufacturers complied. Other fabric companies created lines upon which they could base competitions, presenting a new collection each year. Some unusual participants also entered the market; for example, Hallmark Cards produced a line of Christmas fabric in 1981, and Sears Roebuck & Co. sold a fabric

A Quilting Revival

1987 The AIDS Memorial Quilt is displayed on the National Mall in Washington, D.C.   **1989** The Berlin Wall comes down.

1992 The World Wide Web is born.   **1993** The first issue of *American Patchwork & Quilting* is published; *The Bridges of Madison County* by Robert James Waller is a fiction best-seller.   **1997** *Harry Potter and the Sorcerer's Stone*, the first in a series of popular children's books, is

line with the imprint "A Vincent Price National Treasure." A related trend was fabric to bear the logos and images of brand-name products.

ENDLESS POSSIBILITIES FOR QUILTERS

Quiltmakers tried using all kinds of fabrics. And if they did not find fabrics to buy that suited their needs, they painted, stenciled, crayoned, embroidered, or manipulated to get what they wanted. New and improved quilt batting which required less stitching to hold it in place expanded quilting horizons, too, in creations such as Jackie Curry's machine-quilted quilt made from 12-inch squares, shown *left*. Designers also used their sewing machines for speedy piecing, appliquéing, and quilting.

In the August 1972 issue of Better Homes and Gardens, *Jackie Curry provided readers with a glimpse into the future of quilting.*

Not your great-grandmother's quilt, this sampler from the '70s combines classic blocks in entirely new ways. ORCHID QUILT, c. 1985; 91×103"

Polyester quilt batting made new designs possible, since quilting stitches no longer had to be close together.

published; *Titanic* is the most successful movie ever.   **2000** At age 24, Tiger Woods is the youngest golfer to win the U.S. and British Opens and PGA and Masters tournaments; more than half of American households have a computer. **2001** September 11: World Trade Center towers in New York City collapse in terrorist attack.   **2002** Meredith Corporation celebrates 100 years of publishing.

HOME
FAMILY
MEREDITH

100 Years of Serving
America's Homes and Families

Meredith
CORPORATION

THE *JOURNAL'S* PATCHWORK FASHION

*A*lthough quilts rarely appeared in *Ladies' Home Journal* in the past 30 years, the magazine featured one notable exception in 1972. At the beginning of the 1970s, patchwork was a trendy fashion. In the enthusiasm for the quilt look, fine old quilts and tops were sacrificed for clothes and decorating. A *Ladies' Home Journal* cover in November 1972 showed a dress made from an old quilt top. It was part of "A Potpourri of Patchwork" for Christmas projects that also included a crazy quilt stocking and evening jacket.

The word "patchwork" originally referred to appliqué, but the new quilt era expanded the meaning to include almost anything and everything related to quilts, especially the uniting of smaller geometric shapes into a larger whole. "We use the term patchwork permissively to cover a multitude of beautiful things that range from classic country quilting to contemporary wall hangings," *Ladies' Home Journal* stated. "For materials, track down bits and pieces of old quilts in antique and secondhand stores (they're surprisingly available). Or put all those odd scraps of fabric that have been accumulating to good purpose." The scraps worked up into place mats, neckties, pillows, and ornaments. A variety of self-sticking decorative papers even "patchworked" a small wood table.

BETTER HOMES AND GARDENS CARRIES THE QUILTING TORCH

The tradition of providing instructions and patterns for home crafts the average person could accomplish gave *Better Homes and Gardens* the ideal opportunity to incorporate many aspects of the quilt revival and, in turn, influence millions of readers.

Judging from an absence of quilt-related material in 1970 to the use of something pieced, appliquéd, or quilted in more than half the issues in 1972, it's clear that the magazine was quick to join the quilt revival. A feature about such subjects as a modern quilting bee and a bedspread printed with an antique "Log Cabin" pattern brought patchwork to the attention of a mass audience of more than 7 million subscribers. The frequent appearance of quilts in the magazine paralleled their popularity elsewhere and fostered awareness in those who otherwise might not have been exposed to the craft.

NEW STYLES FOR QUILTS

A cheerful cover on the October 1972 issue of *Better Homes and Gardens, below,* introduced two comical and colorful quilts in the shapes of a lion and an elephant. Designer

Beginning in 1972, Better Homes and Gardens *drastically increased the number of quilting projects in the magazine.*

Donna Beals supplied complete directions for straight-stitch appliqué of the simple shapes cut out of sailcloth, sewing the back to the front for a knife-edge finish, and simple tacking to hold the layers together.

In August 1976 a modern "Butterfly Quilt," shown *above* and *right*, captured the bright side of the 1970s in clear warm hues. The bold butterflies and flowers were the work of Charlotte Patera, a freelance contributor of craft projects to *Better Homes and Gardens*. Charlotte had designed graphics for packages until the mid-1960s. She changed careers when she found that working with thread and fabric expressed her creative ideas and appliqué methods suited her style.

Quiltmaker Maurine Moore adapted the BUTTERFLY QUILT in Better Homes and Gardens, *shown* left, *by adding sashing and borders. c. 1976; 82×105"*

CLASSIC VS. CONTEMPORARY QUILTS

I n May 1978, a *Better Homes and Gardens* editor featured the needlework of a family member in the article "Needlework Treasures from Aunt Mary's." The writer introduced Aunt Mary's collection by saying: "The careful curator of a unique family collection of needlework and antiques, Aunt Mary is always willing to share the delights and treasures of her home. And because we so enjoy our visits to Aunt Mary's house, we have arranged this one for you. Here is a sampling of exquisite needlework—not only for you to see, but also to reproduce for your own home."

One of the quilts included in the article was this appliquéd "Rose Quilt" made by Mary's mother, an aunt, and a neighbor in Redfield, Iowa. This was one of four identical quilts stitched from two shades of elegant pastel pink sateen with a touch of green for the hope chests of four Bennison sisters in the 1920s, just about the time that Carlie Sexton published an identical pattern she called "Ohio Rose." Although similar to a pattern from the early 20th century called "Colonial Rose," the shape of the leaves most closely resembles Carlie's design. *Better Homes and Gardens* included the pattern and directions in the May 1978 issue and produced a kit with precut pieces sold by mail.

In 1974 Charlotte wrote *The Appliqué Book,* published by Creative Home Library for Meredith Corporation, which covered basic information about fabrics and techniques and provided many bold, simple designs often inspired by folk art motifs from around the world.

A January 1981 feature provided a glimpse of a whole family of designers creating a whole raft of crafts. In the Jerdee family, mom Becky sewed, dad Allen worked with wood, and children Adam and Amy contributed drawings and plans. Becky stitched a folk art marriage certificate quilt, shown *opposite,* and added dates of special family events. She also appliquéd Adam's and Amy's drawings on quilts and folk art wall hangings. Instructions encouraged readers to incorporate the work of their children in the same way.

In the July 1981 issue of the magazine, a popular pattern was the "Transportation Quilt," shown *right*. Particularly suitable as a wall hanging in a child's room or as a crib quilt, the project exemplified that almost any theme could be the basis for design motifs.

Quiltmaker Maurine Moore made the TRANSPORTATION QUILT from a pattern featured in Better Homes and Gardens. c. 1990; 49×71"

Opposite: *During the 1980s, appliqué appeared in bold, bright ways on quilts. Becky Jerdee's MARRIAGE QUILT appeared in* Better Homes and Gardens *in 1981; 84×98".*

Better Homes and Gardens magazine and books showed quilters how to update appliqué with brilliant colors and unusual motifs.

WE LOVE QUILTING

The holiday issue of *Better Homes and Gardens*, December 1977, turned out to be a real winner—the best-selling issue ever up to that time. The quilted decorations, pillows, and woman's skirt on the cover appealed to readers. Among a multitude of other projects inside were "portrait pillows," printed from old family photographs.

Talented designers and writers, both freelance and on staff, contributed a variety of popular quilting designs to the pages of *Better Homes and Gardens* during the late 1980s and early 1990s. The July 1988 issue was filled with crafts and quilting patterns. Editors relied quite a bit on developing instructions based on vintage quilts, pleasing the quiltmakers of the 1980s, who found the myriad of small-print cotton fabrics that had come on the market suitable for traditional patterns and styles.

A quilt that combined machine appliqué and embroidery for Garden Alphabet blocks, which contained flowers intertwining with letters, appeared in the March 1990 issue, *right*. Although instructions could be found in the magazine, the mail-order project sparked a lot of response from readers and became a good seller.

Another popular pattern was the "Colors-of-Friendship Quilt," with strip-pieced folk art figures in different sizes representing men, women, and children, shown *above, far right*. Outstretched arms linked the figures, which could be arranged in different family or friendship groups and dressed up with

individualizing details. This quilt was designed by a magazine staff member who also cocreated the "Hearts and Hands Quilt," *opposite*, an adaptation of a crazy quilt without the fancy stitching but with appliquéd antique gloves, for the May 1994 issue.

SOUTHWEST QUILTERS ARE BROADWAY BOUND

In February 1976, *Better Homes and Gardens* introduced the "Southwest Quilters" in a stunning eight-page layout. Beautiful photographs set against the stark landscape of Texas and New Mexico lovingly captured the character of seven women and the quilts that were, the article said, "a record of their lives, loves, hopes and hard times." The article was written by Myles Callum in cooperation with Patricia Cooper and Norma Buferd, whose interviews with Southwest quilters were about to be published by Doubleday as *The Quilters: Women and Domestic Art*. The book won numerous awards and was adapted by Molly Newman and Barbara Damashek into the popular musical drama *The Quilters*, which premiered on Broadway in 1984 and continues to be performed by theater groups around the country.

One of the seven quilters, Mrs. Arthur Woodburn, pieced a star design "Bicentennial Quilt" for *Better Homes and Gardens*, and another, Mabel Metcalf, quilted it. Their red, white, and blue quilt appeared on the February cover. Readers could buy fabrics and follow the pattern and directions provided in the magazine, or they could order a kit for the top and matching pillows. (To make this quilt, see *page 120*.)

HEARTS AND HANDS was crafted by Jilann Severson and Kathy Moore for a 1994 issue of Better Homes and Gardens; *42½×67".*

"A whole new group of women— and, increasingly, men—come to quilting with neither expectations nor preconceptions about the process. One welcome result of this burgeoning interest among non-traditionally trained quilters is an influx of new ideas and new sense of possibilities, both of which keep the craft and art of quilting alive and exciting."
—Ciba Vaughan,
Romantic Patchwork & Quilting, 1989
(distributed by Meredith Corporation)

FARM LIFE, FARM QUILTS

Just as fabric artists at this time used quilts to express ideas and feelings, rural quiltmakers stitched images of the land, farm, and family and captured their memories, experiences, and dreams in cloth. In the 1990s, long after quilting patterns had been discontinued in the magazine, *Successful Farming* published several quilt features, all related to farm and family values.

An imaginative child's bed in the shape of a tractor, *below left*, was designed for the cover of the December 1991 issue and needed—naturally—a farm quilt. Marianne Fons, an

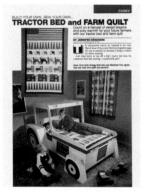

award-winning quilter, writer, and teacher from Winterset, Iowa, designed a top in a popular new format with repeating images lined up one after the other in rows. The editors described the quilt this way: "Our quilt's bright colors and adorable livestock are sure to be a hit with farm kids and their city cousins. The rows of corn, barns, silos, tractors, and a flag round out our picture of everything kids (and parents and grandparents) love about farming."

A month later, the magazine featured Diane Schlagel's "Celebrate Colorado Country" quilt. Diane, a farm wife and quilter in eastern Colorado, made the quilt for an auction to benefit the Colorado Agriculture Leadership Program. Of her passion, she said, "I love the farm, but quilting is something that's me—it's my part of life."

Diane's article apparently touched a chord with other rural quilters. Interest in her quilt prompted *Successful Farming* to invite readers to submit traditional or original farm-related blocks for a quilt intended "to be a picture of agriculture, with a view of the past and vision for the future."

Twenty-nine winning blocks and one title block were assembled into the "Successful Farming Reader Quilt" and published in the October 1992 issue, *right*. Many groups asked to exhibit the quilt, and in the next three years, thousands of people viewed it at county fairs, churches, libraries, schools, offices, museums, and festivals.

BOOKS FOR QUILTERS

As Meredith Corporation grew, it provided helpful information in books, too. About 25 years ago, the first quilt title joined the long list of cooking, decorating, building, and gardening books produced by Meredith Books. Since then, more than 4 million quilting books have been sold—evidence that the renewed interest in quilting sparked by America's Bicentennial celebration was not just a passing fad. In 1977, Meredith Books published *Patchwork and Quilting*, which sold more than 1 million copies. As the quilting audience grew, the company produced single-focused books, such as *Folk Art Quilting* and *Victorian Patchwork & Quilting*, to cater to every kind of quilter. Meanwhile, top sellers such as *American Patchwork & Quilting* and *101 Full-Size Quilt Blocks and Borders* provided traditional quilt patterns and easy-to-follow instructions.

With the interest in quilting still on the rise, Meredith Corporation now publishes two to three quilting books a year, including the latest title, *Grandma's Best Full-Size Quilt Blocks*.

The pages of American Patchwork & Quilting *magazine show that quilts have moved beyond being strictly functional to becoming essential elements in decorating schemes. Quiltmaker and designer Nancy Martin uses a traditional Pine Burr quilt design, stitched in a blue-and-yellow color scheme, as the focal point of her living room.*

A MAGAZINE FOR QUILTERS

As the number of quilters increased in the 1980s, Meredith Corporation realized that quilters wanted more than occasional articles in *Better Homes and Gardens*. In 1993, the company launched *American Patchwork & Quilting* magazine to provide quilters with new patterns and a better understanding of how to make quilts. Ten years later, the magazine has 250,000 subscribers, more than any other quilting magazine.

Additional publications, such as the magazines *Quilting Ideas*® and *Quilt Sampler*™, the book series *Quilt-Lovers' Favorites*™, and the *Celebrate with Quilts*™ calendars are produced to provide quilters more inspiration. In 2002, Meredith published *The Complete Guide to Quilting*™, a complete how-to reference book created to help quilters in the 21st century quilt successfully.

American Patchwork & Quilting showcases new designs while providing quilters with reliable, practical quilting instructions.

INVESTING IN QUILTING'S FUTURE

To ensure the preservation of the art of quilting, *American Patchwork & Quilting* is funding a new research program entitled The Meredith Scholar. In October 2002, $10,000 was given to the American Quilt Study Group based in Lincoln, Nebraska, to support their mission of "establishing, sustaining, and promoting the highest standards for quilt studies." The donation will award an exceptional researcher who provides new knowledge of quilts or textile-related topics.

Georgia Bonesteel

Designers of Today

A wide selection of fabrics, quilting tools, and patterns is available to inspire 21st-century quilters, thanks to the ingenuity of the following women who have been featured in *American Patchwork & Quilting*.

THE TELEVISION QUILTER
GEORGIA BONESTEEL
Creator and host of the public television series *Lap Quilting*, Georgia was one of the first quilters to appear on the small screen. The series, which began airing in 1979, continues to encourage beginning quilters as well as provide tips for accomplished crafters.

Harriet Hargrave

A WHIZ AT MACHINE QUILTING
HARRIET HARGRAVE
Before Harriet entered the quilting scene, machine quilting and piecing was frowned upon by purists. Then Harriet, who learned on a treadle sewing machine, demonstrated a new level of artistry with machine quilting. Her first media tour in 1983 redefined quiltmaking. Quilters realized they no longer had to sew every stitch by hand. Today she is still teaching the joys of machine quilting through lectures, classes, and her books.

Lynette Jensen

Little Quilts partners
Sylvia Johnson, Alice Berg, and Mary Ellen Von Holt

A New Twist on the Traditional
Lynette Jensen

The creative genius behind Thimbleberries quilt patterns and fabrics, Lynette looks to heritage quilts for inspiration. Quilters are drawn to her fabric collections designed around coordinating color palettes and her simple instructions for stunning, doable quilts.

Quilting on a Smaller Scale
Little Quilts

In 1986, three friends discovered a common interest in small quilts made for dolls and began selling ready-made reproduction doll quilts. Calling their business Little Quilts, Alice Berg, Sylvia Johnson, and Mary Ellen Von Holt set off a wave of interest in a new type of decor and quiltmaking. Now they also design patterns for miniature quilts.

Tools of the Trade
Marti Michell

In the 1960s when Marti taught quilting classes, there was very little 100-percent cotton fabric available, so she made her own kits. Over the years, she has focused on providing products that make quilting easier. Today she sells acrylic templates and patterns to use in conjunction with rotary cutters for fast, accurate piecing.

Quilting as Interior Design
Debbie Mumm

Debbie made her first quilt, a "Double Irish Chain," in the early 1980s. The next quilt—and every quilt she's made since—was her own design. She's taken the art one step further to design accessories, fabrics, and home decor items to coordinate with her quilt designs. Specialty items, from candle toppers to kitchen products, reflect the traditional, yet contemporary look that is her distinctive style.

A passion for quilting and for sharing their talents with others has brought these women to the forefront of America's renewed interest in quilting. Their creative visions will continue to inspire quilters in the 21st century.

Marti Michell

Debbie Mumm

A Century *of* Projects

For 100 years, readers have been inspired to make quilts that have appeared in Meredith magazines. Choose from our selection of classic designs made in today's fabrics to re-create a charming quilt with a history. Our up-to-date instructions begin on page 88.

1902–1919

1920–1929

1930-1939

1940-1969

1970-2002

Spring Flowers

Noted designer Marie Webster presented "Field Daisies" and "Tulip"
as chair cushions in the August 1911 issue of Ladies' Home Journal.
Nowadays they're colorful accent pillows for your home.

A quilt contributor to Ladies' Home
Journal *for more than 15 years, Marie
Webster also designed the cushions that
inspired these pillows (see third row,
right and bottom row, left).*

TULIP PILLOW MATERIALS

1 yard of solid blue for appliqué
    foundation, pillow backing, and
    cording cover
⅛ yard of solid green for appliqués
⅛ yard of solid yellow for appliqués
18" square of quilt batting
18" square of muslin for pillow top lining
2 yards of ¼" cotton cording
14" square pillow form

Finished pillow: 14" square

Quantities specified for 44/45"-wide
100% cotton fabrics. All measurements
include a ¼" seam allowance.
Sew with right sides together unless
otherwise stated.

CUT THE FABRICS

To make the best use of your fabrics, cut
the pieces in the order that follows. The
patterns are on *page 136*. To make templates of
the patterns, follow the instructions in Quilter's
Schoolhouse, which begins on *page 131*.

The appliqué foundation is cut larger than
necessary to allow for sewing differences.
You'll trim the foundation to the correct size
after completing the appliqué and quilting.

When cutting out appliqué pieces, add a
³⁄₁₆" seam allowance.

From solid blue, cut:
- 1—18" square for appliqué foundation
- 1—18" square, cutting it into enough 1½"-wide bias strips to total 72" in length for cording cover (For specific instructions on cutting bias strips, see Quilter's Schoolhouse.)
- 1—15" square for pillow back

From solid green, cut:
- 4 *each* of patterns A, A reversed, B, B reversed, and C

From solid yellow, cut:
- 12 of Pattern D

PREPARE THE PILLOW TOP

1. Referring to the Tulip Pillow Appliqué Placement Diagram, position the appliqué pieces on the solid blue 18" square; baste in place.

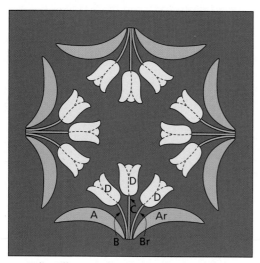

Tulip Pillow Appliqué Placement Diagram

2. Using threads in colors that match the fabrics, appliqué each piece to the foundation, turning the edges under with your needle as you work. You do not need to turn under edges that will be overlapped by other pieces. In the case of extremely small pieces, you may need to trim away part of the seam allowance. Begin with the pieces on the bottom and work up.

3. When you've completed the appliqué, press the appliquéd foundation from the back on a soft surface, such as a folded towel.

4. Layer the appliquéd foundation, batting, and lining according to the instructions in Quilter's Schoolhouse, which begins on *page 131.*

5. Quilt the pillow top as desired. Quilter Ruth Smith outlined each flower motif and quilted in the center of each tulip to create petals. In the center of the pillow top, she quilted three squares with convex sides, each ½" apart.

COMPLETE THE PILLOW

1. Trim the appliquéd and quilted pillow top so it measures 14½" square, including the seam allowances.

2. Make the cording cover from the solid blue 1½"-wide bias strips according to the instructions in Quilter's Schoolhouse, which begins on *page 131.* Sew cording to the pillow top according to the directions in Quilter's Schoolhouse.

3. With wrong sides together, layer the pillow top and pillow back. Fold the cording seam allowance between the layers. Fold under the pillow back edges ½". (The seam allowance is deeper for the pillow back to make hand stitching easier.) Whipstitch the edges together to make the pillow cover, leaving an 8 to 10" opening. Insert the pillow form in the pillow cover. Whipstitch the opening closed.

DAISY PILLOW MATERIALS

⅝ yard of solid green for appliqué
    foundation and pillow backing
⅝ yard of solid dark green for appliqués
    and cording cover
⅛ yard of solid white for appliqués
Scrap of solid yellow for appliqués
18" square of quilt batting
18" square of muslin for pillow top lining
2 yards of ¼" cotton cording
14" square pillow form

Finished pillow: 14" square

Quantities specified for 44/45"-wide
100% cotton fabrics. All measurements
include a ¼" seam allowance.
Sew with right sides together unless
otherwise stated.

CUT THE FABRICS

To make the best use of your fabrics, cut the
pieces in the order that follows. The patterns
are on *page 136*. To make templates of the
patterns, follow the instructions in Quilter's
Schoolhouse, which begins on *page 131*.

The appliqué foundation is cut larger than
necessary to allow for sewing differences. You'll
trim the foundation to the correct size after
completing the appliqué and quilting.

When cutting out appliqué pieces, add a
³⁄₁₆" seam allowance.

From solid green, cut:
- 1—18" square for appliqué foundation
- 1—15" square for pillow back

From solid dark green, cut:
- 1—18" square, cutting it into enough
  1½"-wide bias strips to total 72" in length for
  cording cover (For specific instructions on
  cutting bias strips, see Quilter's Schoolhouse.)
- 4 of Pattern E

From solid white, cut:
- 4 *each* of patterns F, G, and H

From solid yellow, cut:
- 4 of Pattern I

PREPARE THE PILLOW TOP

1. Referring to the Daisy Pillow Appliqué
Placement Diagram and Prepare the Pillow
Top, steps 1 through 4, *opposite*, make a daisy
pillow top.

Daisy Pillow Appliqué Placement Diagram

2. Quilt the pillow top as desired. Quilter Ruth
Smith outlined each daisy motif and quilted a
series of eight 1½"-diameter overlapping circles
in the center of the pillow top.

COMPLETE THE PILLOW

Trim the appliquéd and quilted pillow top
to measure 14½" square, including the seam
allowances. Make and sew on the cording and
sew the pillow top and backing together
according to the directions in Complete the
Pillow, *opposite*.

Windmill Quilt

In 1903, when this pattern appeared in the April issue of Ladies' Home Journal, two-color quilts of red and white were highly prized. Instead of using white, we offset the red whirligigs with cream-and-black shirting prints.

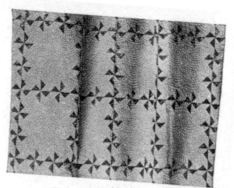

THE WINDMILL PATTERN

MATERIALS

6½ yards total of assorted cream shirting prints for blocks, setting squares and units, and borders
1¾ yards of red print for blocks and pieced border
⅝ yard of red-and-black print for binding
5 yards of backing fabric
72×89" of quilt batting

Finished quilt top: 65¼×82⅛"
Finished block: 12" square

Quantities specified for 44/45"-wide, 100% cotton fabrics. All measurements include a ¼" seam allowance.
Sew with right sides together unless otherwise stated.

CUT THE FABRICS

To make the best use of your fabrics, cut the pieces in the order that follows. There are no pattern pieces for this project; the letter designations are for placement only. The border strips are cut the length (parallel to the selvage) of the fabric.

From assorted cream shirting prints, cut:
• 4—2×88" border strips
• 4—2×72" border strips
• 12—12½" setting squares
• 11—7" squares, cutting each diagonally twice in an X for a total of 44 C triangles (you'll have two leftover triangles)
• 48—4½" B squares
• 25—4⅛" squares, cutting each diagonally twice in an X for a total of 100 E triangles
• 2—3¾" squares, cutting each in half diagonally for a total of 4 D triangles
• 164—2⅞" squares, cutting each in half diagonally for a total of 328 A triangles
From red print, cut:
• 24—4⅛" squares, cutting each diagonally twice in an X for a total of 96 E triangles
• 164—2⅞" squares, cutting each in half diagonally for a total of 328 A triangles
From red-and-black print, cut:
• 8—2½×42" binding strips

ASSEMBLE THE PINWHEEL UNITS

1. Sew together one cream print A triangle and one red print A triangle to make a triangle-square (see Diagram 1). Press the seam allowance toward the red triangle. The pieced triangle-square should measure 2½" square, including the seam allowances. Repeat to make a total of 328 triangle-squares.

Diagram 1

2. Referring to Diagram 2 for placement, sew together four triangle-squares in pairs. Press the seam allowances toward the red triangles. Then join the pairs to make one Pinwheel unit. Press the seam allowance in one direction. The pieced Pinwheel unit should measure 4½" square, including the seam allowances. Repeat to make a total of 82 Pinwheel units.

Diagram 2

ASSEMBLE THE WINDMILL BLOCKS

1. Referring to Diagram 3 for placement, lay out five Pinwheel units and four cream print B squares in three rows.

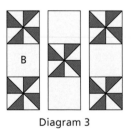

Diagram 3

2. Sew together the pieces in each row. Press the seam allowances toward the cream squares. Then join the rows to make a Windmill block. Press the seam allowances in one direction. The pieced Windmill block should measure 12½" square, including the seam allowances.

3. Repeat steps 1 and 2 to make a total of six Windmill blocks.

ASSEMBLE THE SIDE SETTING UNITS

1. Referring to Diagram 4 for placement, sew together four Pinwheel units, two cream print B squares, and three cream print C triangles in diagonal rows. Press the seam allowances in one direction, alternating the direction with each row.

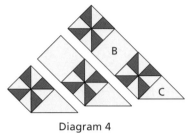

Diagram 4

2. Join the rows to make a side setting unit A. Press the seam allowances in one direction.

3. Repeat steps 1 and 2 to make a total of six of side setting unit A.

4. Referring to Diagram 5 for placement, sew together four Pinwheel units, two cream print B squares, and three cream print C triangles in diagonal rows. Press the seam allowances in one direction, alternating the direction with each row.

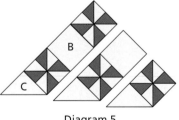

Diagram 5

5. Join the rows to make a side setting unit B. Press the seam allowances in one direction.

6. Repeat steps 4 and 5 to make a total of four of side setting unit B.

ASSEMBLE THE CORNER SETTING UNITS

1. Referring to Diagram 6 for placement, sew together three Pinwheel units, one cream print B square, four cream print C triangles, and one cream print D triangle in diagonal rows. Press the seam allowances toward the cream print square and triangles.

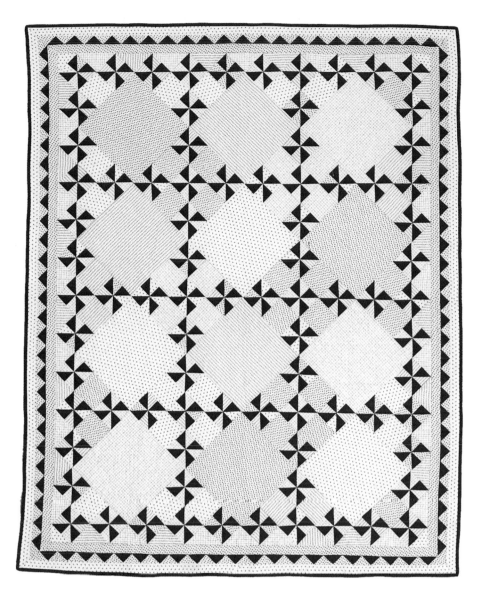

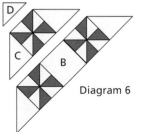

Diagram 6

cream print D triangle in diagonal rows. Press the seam allowances toward the cream print square and triangles.

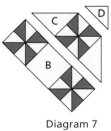

Diagram 7

2. Join the rows to make a corner unit A. Press the seam allowances in one direction.

3. Repeat steps 1 and 2 to make a total of two of corner unit A.

4. Referring to Diagram 7 for placement, sew together three Pinwheel units, one cream print B square, two cream print C triangles, and one

5. Join the rows to make a corner unit B. Press the seam allowances in one direction.

6. Repeat steps 4 and 5 to make a total of two of corner unit B.

ASSEMBLE THE QUILT CENTER

1. Referring to the Quilt Assembly Diagram at *right* for placement, lay out the six Windmill blocks, 12 cream print 12½" setting squares, the side setting units, and the corner units in diagonal rows.

2. Sew together the pieces in diagonal rows; do not add the corner units. Press the seam allowances toward the setting squares. Join the rows. Press the seam allowances in one direction. Add the corner units to complete the quilt center. The pieced quilt center should measure 56¾×73⅝", including the seam allowances.

ASSEMBLE AND ADD THE BORDER

1. Referring to Diagram 8, sew together 21 red print E triangles and 22 cream print E triangles to make a pieced top border strip. Press the seam allowances toward the red triangles. Repeat to make a pieced bottom border strip.

Diagram 8

2. Center and sew a cream print 2×72" strip to each long edge of the pieced top border strip (see Diagram 9). Press the seam allowances toward the cream print strips. Trim the edges for making mitered corners. Repeat to make the bottom border.

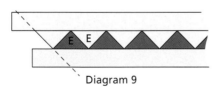

Diagram 9

3. Sew together 27 red print E triangles and 28 cream print E triangles to make a side pieced border strip. Press the seam allowances toward the red print triangles. Repeat to make a second side pieced border strip.

4. Center and sew a cream print 2×88" strip to each long edge of the pieced side border strips. Press the seam allowances toward the cream print strips. Trim the edges for making mitered corners.

Quilt Assembly Diagram

5. Add the pieced borders to the pieced quilt center, mitering the corners to complete the quilt top. For more information on mitering, see Quilter's Schoolhouse, which begins on *page 131*.

COMPLETE THE QUILT

1. Layer the quilt top, batting, and backing according to the instructions in Quilter's Schoolhouse, which begins on *page 131*.

2. Quilt as desired. Quiltmaker Monica Hofer machine-quilted variations of feathered stars in the cream print areas of the quilt and stitched inside each of the red print triangles.

3. Use the red-and-black print 2½×42" strips to bind the quilt according to the instructions in Quilter's Schoolhouse.

Blooming Delight

A design for a hooked rug in the September 1929 issue of
Successful Farming *provided the inspiration for a decorative table piece.*
Hand-dyed felted wool adds a richness to the hand-appliqué project.

In the Successful Farming *magazine feature, designer Laura Holmes extolled the virtue of "old-fashioned" rug-hooking bees. "In our grandmothers' day, it was as popular as the sewing or afternoon club is today, and twice as profitable," she said.*

MATERIALS

18×25" of navy felted wool for appliqué foundation and appliqués

16×24" of blue felted wool for appliqués

15×22" of khaki-gold felted wool for appliqué

5" square of bright gold felted wool for appliqués

16" square of green felted wool for appliqués

4" square of red felted wool for appliqués

Perle cotton: navy, light blue, gold, dark green, and red

Finished tabletop rug: 16½×24"

CUT THE FABRICS

To make the best use of your fabrics, cut the pieces in the order that follows. The patterns are on *pages 140–142*. To make templates of the patterns, follow the instructions in Quilter's Schoolhouse, which begins on *page 131*. It is not necessary to add seam allowances to the appliqué pieces since there are no edges to turn under. Cut the edges cleanly, keeping them as smooth as possible.

From navy wool, cut:
- 1 *each* of patterns A and R
- 26 of Pattern U

From blue wool, cut:
- 1 *each* of patterns B and Q

From khaki-gold wool, cut:
- 1 of Pattern C

From bright gold wool, cut:
- 1 *each* of patterns D, D reversed, and T

From green wool, cut:
- 1 of Pattern E
- 1 *each* of patterns G and G reversed
- 1 *each* of patterns H and H reversed
- 1 *each* of patterns I and I reversed
- 1 *each* of patterns J and J reversed
- 1 *each* of patterns K and K reversed
- 1 *each* of patterns L and L reversed
- 1 *each* of patterns M and M reversed
- 1 *each* of patterns N and N reversed
- 1 *each* of patterns O and O reversed
- 1 *each* of patterns P and P reversed

From red wool, cut:
- 7 of Pattern F
- 1 of Pattern S

APPLIQUÉ AND EMBROIDER THE TABLETOP RUG

1. Referring to the photograph *opposite* and the Appliqué Placement Diagram on *page 142*, lay the blue B border piece on the navy A background piece (see Diagram 1). Baste in place. Using one strand of navy perle cotton, blanket-stitch around the outer edge of the B border, stitching through all layers.

To blanket-stitch, first pull the needle up at A (see diagram *below*). Form a reverse L shape with the thread, and hold the angle of the L shape in place with your thumb. Push the needle down at B and come up at C to secure the stitch. Repeat until you've stitched around the shape.

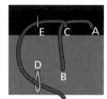

Blanket Stitch

2. Using one strand of light blue perle cotton, stem-stitch around the inner scalloped edge of the blue B border, stitching through all layers.

To stem-stitch, pull the needle up at A. Insert the needle into the fabric at B, about ⅜" away from A (see diagram *below*). Holding the thread out of the way, bring the needle back up at C and pull the thread through so it lies flat against the fabric. The distances between points A, B, and C should be equal. Pull with equal tautness after each stitch.

Stem Stitch

3. Referring to the photograph and placement diagram, lay the khaki-gold C background on the navy wool (see Diagram 2); baste in place.

Diagram 1

Diagram 2

4. Referring to the photograph and placement diagram, lay the green E piece on the navy and khaki-gold wool (see Diagram 3). Arrange gold pieces D and D reversed under piece E. When pleased with the arrangement, baste the gold appliqué pieces in place. With one strand of gold perle cotton, use the herringbone stitch to attach the gold leaves to the khaki-gold piece.

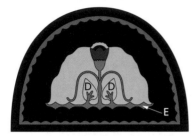

Diagram 3

To herringbone-stitch, pull the needle up at A, then push it down at B (see diagram *below*). Bring the needle up at C, cross over the first stitch, and push the needle down at D. Bring the needle up at E, cross over the second stitch and push the needle down at F.

Using one strand of dark green perle cotton, blanket-stitch around the outer edges of the E piece; herringbone-stitch narrow portions of the stem.

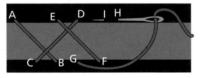

Herringbone Stitch

Place pieces Q, R, S, and T on the khaki-gold wool (see the Blossom Appliqué Placement Diagram on *page 142*); baste in place. Use coordinating perle cotton to stitch the pieces. Herringbone-stitch and blanket-stitch the blue stem. Herringbone-stitch the navy flower. Blanket-stitch the red and gold flowers.

5. Referring to the photograph and the placement diagram, lay the remaining pieces in place; baste. Appliqué as follows:

Using one strand of dark green perle cotton, blanket-stitch the leaves.

Using one strand of red perle cotton, work 17 French knots through the navy background at the top of the center flower.

To make a French knot, pull the perle cotton through at A, the point where the knot is desired (see diagram *below*). Wrap the thread around the needle two times. Insert the tip of the needle into the fabric at B, $\frac{1}{16}$" away from A. Gently pull the wraps down the needle to meet the fabric. Pull the needle and trailing thread through the fabric slowly and smoothly.

French Knot

Using one strand of red perle cotton, blanket-stitch the red F circles to the green E piece. Work a French knot at the center of each circle.

Using one strand of navy perle cotton, blanket-stitch around the outside edges of the navy wool background, as quiltmaker Mary Pepper did, to finish the tabletop rug.

QUILTING WITH WOOL

For warmth, durability, and richness of color, you can't beat wool in quilts. Quilting with wool is not a new technique. In the early 1900s, contributors to *Successful Farming* magazine described quilts made of large squares or rectangles cut from used clothing. Quilters also frequently used salesmen's samples of men's suitings to make utilitarian bedcovers, brightening them with red embroidery over the seam lines or red ties that held the layers together.

Many of today's wool projects use felted wool. This is wool that has been soaked, heated, agitated, and pressed so the fibers are locked together to create a dense fabric that will not fray. To felt wool, machine-wash wool in the hottest water with the longest agitation, then machine-dry at the hottest temperature and steam-press.

Pastel Petals

Adapted from a mail-order quilt block pattern that appeared in a 1927 issue of Better Homes and Gardens, *this table runner teams a vintage appliqué design with modern machine embroidery. We recreated the pattern in colors popular during the early 1900s.*

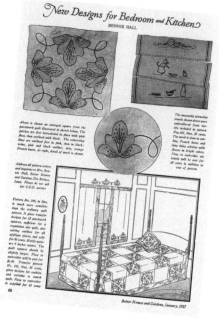

We eliminated the French knots when we updated this appliqué quilt block from a 1927 issue of Better Homes and Gardens.

MATERIALS

¾ yard of solid white for appliqué
    foundation and outer border
⅛ yard of green print for inner border
18×22" piece (fat quarter) *each* of solid
    salmon, solid pink, solid yellow, solid
    lavender, and solid green for flower
    and leaf appliqués
½ yard of backing fabric
½ yard of flannel for batting
Machine embroidery thread in colors
    to match appliqués
Freezer paper (optional)
Fabric glue stick (optional)

Finished table runner: 12×30"

Quantities specified for 44/45"-wide,
100% cotton fabrics. All measurements
include a ¼" seam allowance.
Sew with right sides together unless
otherwise stated.

CUT THE FABRICS

To make the best use of your fabrics, cut the pieces in the order that follows.

The appliqué foundation is cut larger than necessary to allow for sewing differences. You'll trim the foundation to the correct size after completing the appliqué and quilting.

From solid white, cut:
- 1—16×34" rectangle for appliqué foundation
- 2—1¾×28" outer border strips
- 2—1¾×12½" outer border strips

From green print, cut:
- 2—¾×27½" inner border strips
- 2—¾×10" inner border strips

APPLIQUÉ THE TABLE RUNNER

The instructions that follow use freezer paper to prepare the pieces for appliquéing. The pieces can be appliquéd to the foundation either by hand or by machine. If you prefer, another appliqué method may be used. The patterns are on *pages 138 and 139*.

1. Position the freezer paper, shiny side down, over the patterns. With a pencil, trace each pattern the number of times indicated *below*. Cut out the freezer-paper templates on the drawn lines.

From solid salmon, solid pink, solid yellow, and solid lavender, cut:
- 12 of Pattern A (3 of *each* color)

From solid green, cut:
- 12 *each* of patterns B and B reversed

2. Place a small amount of fabric glue on the matte side of the freezer-paper templates and anchor them to the backs of the designated fabrics, leaving approximately ½" between templates for the seam allowances. Cut out the fabric shapes about ¼" beyond the freezer-paper edges.

3. Use the point of a hot, dry iron to press under the seam allowances of the appliqué pieces. Clip curves as necessary.

4. Referring to the photograph on *page 101* and the Pastel Petals Full-Size Pattern Placement Diagram on *page 139* for placement, arrange the prepared appliqué pieces on the solid white 16×34" appliqué foundation. Baste the pieces in place.

5. Working from the bottom layer to the top, use matching thread and your favorite hand or machine appliqué method to stitch each appliqué piece in place, keeping in mind that you'll need to remove the templates. (For hand appliqué, leave a ½" opening along an edge of each piece.) Quiltmaker Patty Edmond machine-blanket-stitched around her appliqué pieces.

6. Remove the freezer-paper templates.

For hand appliqué, use the end of your needle to gently loosen the freezer-paper templates and pull them through the openings. Hand-stitch the openings closed.

For machine appliqué, trim away the foundation behind the appliqués, leaving ¼" seam allowances. With your fingertip or the end of your needle, loosen the freezer-paper templates and gently peel them away from the fabrics.

7. Straight-stitch curlicue vines and the lines within the appliqué flowers and leaves to complete the appliquéd quilt center.

8. Trim the appliquéd quilt center so it measures 9½×27½", including the seam allowances.

ADD THE BORDERS

1. Sew the green print ¾×27½" inner border strips to the long edges of the quilt center. Then join the green print ¾×10" inner border strips to the short edges of the quilt center. Press all seam allowances toward the inner border.

COLOR OPTION

Quilt tester Laura Boehnke selected autumn colors for a country look and set off the golden tones with a narrow purple inner border. By using patterned fabrics for the flowers and petals, she eliminated the need to stitch inside the appliqué pieces.

2. Sew the solid white 1¾×28" outer border strips to the long edges of the quilt center. Then join the solid white 1¾×12½" outer border strips to the short edges of the quilt center to complete the quilt top. Press all seam allowances toward the outer border.

COMPLETE THE TABLE RUNNER

1. Place the backing and quilt top with right sides together. Lay the flannel backing atop the layered pieces. Sew together, leaving a 5"-wide opening for turning. Turn right side out. Slip-stitch the opening closed; press.

2. Quilt as desired. This table runner was quilted in the ditch between the inner and outer borders.

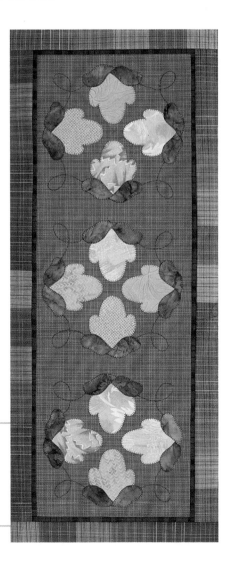

Star Diamond

This classic quilt block appeared in the April 1933 issue of Ladies' Home Journal.

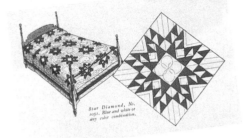

Star Diamond, No. 1051. Blue and white or any color combination.

MATERIALS

7 yards of solid off-white for blocks
    and borders
1½ yards of solid blue for blocks
    and binding
2¾ yards of blue floral for blocks
    and border
7¼ yards of backing fabric
86×106" of quilt batting

Finished quilt top: 80×100"
Finished block: 18" square

Quantities specified for 44/45"-wide,
100% cotton fabrics. All measurements
include a ¼" seam allowance.
Sew with right sides together unless
otherwise stated.

CUT THE FABRICS

To make the best use of your fabrics, cut the pieces in the order that follows. All borders are cut on the lengthwise grain of the fabric (parallel to the selvage). There are no pattern pieces for this project; the letter designations are for placement only.

From solid off-white, cut:
- 2—3½×100½" outer border strips
- 2—3½×74½" outer border strips
- 2—5½×88½" inner border strips
- 2—5½×58½" inner border strips
- 3—2½×58½" sashing strips
- 12—7¼" squares, cutting each diagonally twice in an X for a total of 48 triangles for position F
- 12—6½" squares for position H
- 48—4½" squares for position C
- 24—4¼" squares, cutting each diagonally twice in an X for a total of 96 triangles for position D
- 96—2⅞" squares, cutting each in half diagonally for a total of 192 triangles for position A
- 48—2⅝" squares for position E
- 48—2½" squares for position B
- 8—2½×18½" sashing strips

From solid blue, cut:
- 9—2½×42" binding strips
- 48—3⅞" squares, cutting each in half diagonally for a total of 96 triangles for position G

From blue floral, cut:
- 2—3½×94½" middle border strips
- 2—3½×68½" middle border strips
- 48—4¼" squares, cutting each diagonally twice in an X for a total of 192 triangles for position D
- 96—2⅞" squares, cutting each in half diagonally for a total of 192 triangles for position A

ASSEMBLE UNIT 1

1. For one Unit 1 you'll need four solid off-white A triangles, four blue floral A triangles, one solid off-white B square, and one solid off-white C square.

2. Sew together one solid off-white A triangle and one blue floral A triangle to make a

triangle-square (see Diagram 1). Press the seam allowance toward the blue floral triangle. The pieced triangle-square should measure 2½" square, including the seam allowances. Repeat to make a total of four triangle-squares.

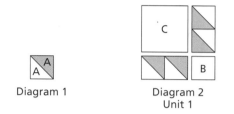

Diagram 1

Diagram 2
Unit 1

3. Referring to Diagram 2 for placement, lay out the four triangle-squares, one B square, and one C square in two rows. Sew together the pieces in each row. Press the seam allowances toward the B and C squares. Then join the rows to make Unit 1. Press the seam allowances in one direction. Pieced Unit 1 should measure 6½" square, including the seam allowances.

4. Repeat steps 1 through 3 to make a total of 48 of Unit 1.

ASSEMBLE UNIT 2

1. For one Unit 2 you'll need four blue floral D triangles, two solid off-white D triangles, one solid off-white E square, one solid off-white F triangle, and two solid blue G triangles.

2. Join one solid off-white D triangle and one blue floral D triangle to make a triangle-square. The triangle-square should measure 2⅝" square, including the seam allowances. Repeat to make a second triangle-square.

3. Referring to Diagram 3 for placement, lay out the two triangle-squares, two blue floral D triangles, one solid off-white E square, and one solid off-white F triangle in diagonal rows. Sew together the pieces in each row. Press the seam allowances toward the off-white E and F pieces.

Diagram 3

Diagram 4
Unit 2

Then join the rows. Press the seam allowances in one direction.

4. Referring to Diagram 4 for placement, join the two solid blue G triangles to adjoining side edges of the Step 3 unit to make Unit 2. Press the seam allowances toward the large triangles. Pieced Unit 2 should measure 6½" square, including the seam allowances.

5. Repeat steps 1 through 4 to make a total of 48 of Unit 2.

ASSEMBLE THE STAR DIAMOND BLOCKS

1. Referring to Diagram 5 for placement, lay out four of Unit 1, four of Unit 2, and one solid off-white H square in three horizontal rows of three units each.

Diagram 5

2. Sew together the units in each row. Press the seam allowances in one direction, alternating with each row. Then join the rows to make a Star Diamond block. Press the seam allowances in one direction. The pieced Star Diamond block should measure 18½" square, including the seam allowances.

3. Repeat steps 1 and 2 to make a total of 12 Star Diamond blocks.

ASSEMBLE THE QUILT CENTER

1. Referring to the Quilt Assembly Diagram for placement, lay out the 12 Star Diamond blocks, the eight off-white 2½×18½" sashing strips, and the three off-white 2½×58½" sashing strips in seven horizontal rows.

2. Sew together the pieces in each row. Press all seam allowances toward the sashing strips. Then join the rows to make the quilt center. Press the seam allowances in one direction. The pieced quilt center should measure 58½×78½", including the seam allowances.

ADD THE BORDERS

1. Sew the solid off-white 5½×58½" inner border strips to the top and bottom edges of the pieced quilt center. Then add the solid off-white 5½×88½" inner border strips to the side edges of the pieced quilt center. Press the seam allowances toward the solid off-white border.

2. Sew the blue floral 3½×68½" middle border strips to the top and bottom edges of the pieced quilt center. Then add the blue floral 3½×94½" middle border strips to the side edges of the pieced quilt center. Press the seam allowances toward the blue print border.

3. Sew the solid off-white 3½×74½" outer border strips to the top and bottom edges of the pieced quilt center. Then add the solid off-white 3½×100½" outer border strips to the side edges of the pieced quilt center to complete the quilt top. Press the seam allowances toward the blue print border.

COMPLETE THE QUILT TOP

1. Layer the quilt top, batting, and backing according to the instructions in Quilter's Schoolhouse, which begins on *page 131*.

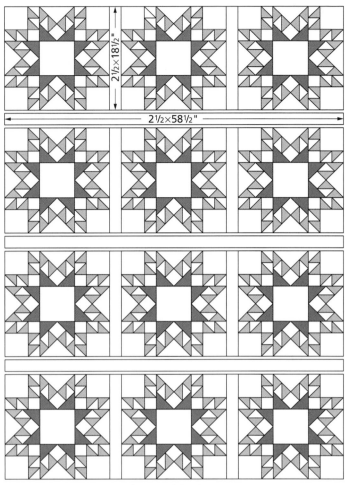

Quilt Assembly Diagram

2. Quilt as desired. Quilter Sally Terry machine-quilted around each piece in the Star Diamond block and diagonally in the center. In the center of each large off-white area, she stitched overlapping circles. For the outer off-white border, she quilted half circles.

3. Use the solid blue 2½×42" strips to bind the quilt according to the instructions in Quilter's Schoolhouse.

COLOR OPTION

Patriotic-print flannel shows off the complex piecing of this block. To frame the block, quilt tester Laura Boehnke added sashing squares to sashing strips. With borders, the block is the perfect size for a floor cushion or a small wall hanging.

Eight-Point All-Over

This crib quilt is based on a design popular in the late 1800s. The easy-to-piece block was introduced to Better Homes and Gardens *readers in 1932 by Emma Tyrrell and Ruby Short McKim.*

MATERIALS

1½ yards total of assorted pink prints for blocks

1½ yards of solid cream for blocks and binding

1½ yards of solid pink for blocks

1½ yards of backing fabric

42×51" of quilt batting

Finished quilt top: 36×45"
Finished block: 3" square

Quantities specified for 44/45"-wide, 100% cotton fabrics. All measurements include a ¼" seam allowance. Sew with right sides together unless otherwise stated.

CUT THE FABRICS

To make the best use of your fabrics, cut the pieces in the order that follows.

From assorted pink prints, cut:
• 180—3½" squares

From solid cream, cut:
• 5—2½×42" binding strips
• 360—2" squares

From solid pink, cut:
• 360—2" squares

ASSEMBLE BLOCK A

1. For one Block A you'll need one assorted pink print 3½" square and four solid pink 2" squares.

2. For accurate sewing lines, use a quilter's pencil to mark a diagonal line on the wrong side of each solid pink 2" square. (To prevent your fabric from stretching as you draw the lines, place 220-grit sandpaper under the squares.)

3. Align two marked solid pink 2" squares with opposite corners of the assorted pink print

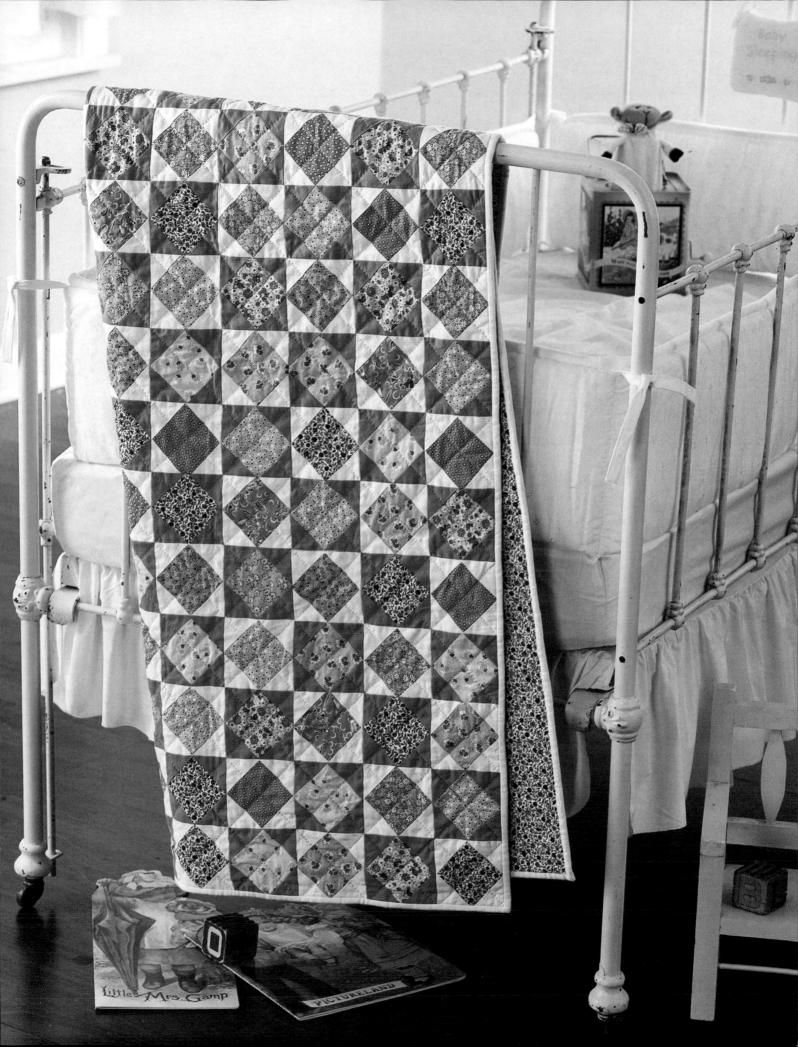

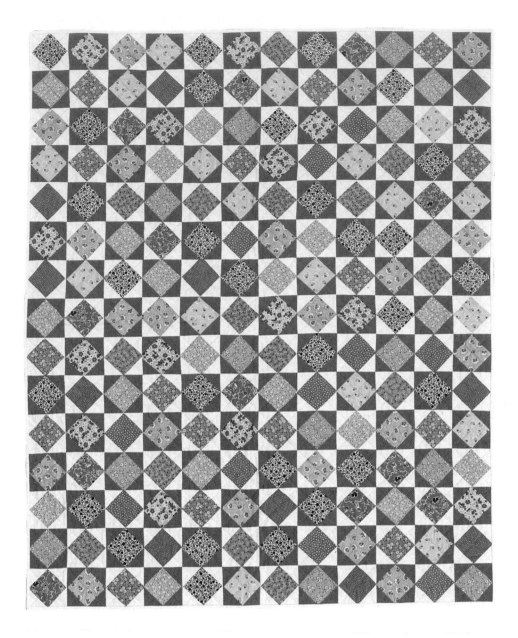

3½" square (see Diagram 1; note the placement of the marked diagonal lines). Stitch on the marked lines; trim the seam allowances to ¼". Press the attached triangles open.

4. Align two marked solid pink 2" squares with the remaining corners of the pink print square (see Diagram 2; note the placement of the marked diagonal lines). Stitch on the marked lines; trim the seam allowances and press the triangles open as before to make a Block A. Pieced Block A should measure 3½" square, including the seam allowances.

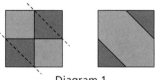

Diagram 1

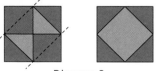

Diagram 2

5. Repeat steps 1 through 4 to make a total of 90 of Block A.

ASSEMBLE BLOCK B

1. For one Block B you'll need one assorted pink print 3½" square and four solid cream 2" squares.

2. Mark a diagonal line on the wrong side of the solid cream 2" squares as before.

3. Align two marked solid cream 2" squares with opposite corners of the assorted pink print 3½" square (see Diagram 3; note the placement of the marked diagonal lines). Stitch, trim, and press as before.

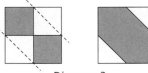

Diagram 3

4. Align two marked solid cream 2" squares with the remaining corners of the pink print square (see Diagram 4; note the placement of the marked diagonal lines). Stitch, trim, and press as before to make a Block B. Pieced Block B should measure 3½" square, including the seam allowances.

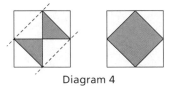

Diagram 4

5. Repeat steps 1 through 4 to make a total of 90 of Block B.

ASSEMBLE THE QUILT TOP

1. Referring to the photograph *opposite* for placement, lay out the 90 A blocks and the 90 B blocks in 15 horizontal rows, alternating blocks A and B as shown.

2. Sew together the blocks in each horizontal row. Press the seam allowances toward the A blocks. Then join the rows to make the quilt top. Press the seam allowances in one direction.

COMPLETE THE QUILT

1. Layer the quilt top, batting, and backing according to the instructions in Quilter's Schoolhouse, which begins on *page 131*.

2. Quilt as desired. Quilter Kathleen Williams hand-quilted the crib quilt by simply stitching through the middle of each block in both directions.

3. Use the solid cream 2½×42" strips to bind the quilt according to the instructions in Quilter's Schoolhouse.

BACK TO THE '30s
WITH JUDIE ROTHERMEL

Virtually everyone has a memory of the pastel print fabrics of the 1930s, whether from an old dress or heirloom quilt. With her collection of 1930s reproduction fabrics, designer Judie Rothermel has provided quilters a way to create the looks of their grandmothers' and great-grandmothers' quilts.

Hired as a designer for Marcus Brothers Textiles in 1987, Judie based her first line, The Centennial Collection, on the 1840s to 1880s fabrics that are her first love. Four years later, she introduced the Aunt Grace collection of charming 1930s prints that she's been designing ever since. Named to honor her Great-Great Aunt Grace with whom Judie quilted, the collection contains all original designs inspired by antique textiles, not remakes of old prints.

Geometric Puzzle

One of the blocks that appeared in the April 1943 issue of Successful Farming *makes a dramatic statement in this quilt. Back then, patterns were sold by mail order.*

MATERIALS

5 yards of muslin for blocks, setting squares and triangles, and outer border

2 yards of solid orange for blocks and binding

1 yard of orange print for blocks and inner border

5 yards of backing fabric

71×90" of quilt batting

Finished quilt top: 64⅜×83½"

Finished block: 13½" square

Quantities specified for 44/45"-wide, 100% cotton fabrics. All measurements include a ¼" seam allowance. Sew with right sides together unless otherwise stated.

CUT THE FABRICS

To make the best use of your fabrics, cut the pieces in the order that follows.

From muslin, cut:

- 7—3×42" strips for outer border
- 12—2×42" strips
- 3—20⅜" squares, cutting each diagonally twice in an X for a total of 12 side setting triangles (you'll have 2 leftover triangles)
- 6—14" setting squares
- 2—10½" squares, cutting each in half diagonally for a total of 4 corner triangles
- 216—2⅜" squares, cutting each in half diagonally for a total of 432 small triangles
- 12—3½" squares
- 4—4" squares for border corners

From solid orange, cut:

- 8—2½×42" binding strips
- 216—2⅜" squares, cutting each in half diagonally for a total of 432 small triangles
- 24—1¼×5" rectangles
- 24—1¼×3½" rectangles

From orange print, cut:

- 6—2×42" strips
- 7—1½×42" strips for inner border

ASSEMBLE THE UNITS

Triangle Units

1. Sew together one muslin small triangle and one solid orange small triangle to make a triangle-square (see Diagram 1). Press the seam allowance toward the orange triangle. The pieced triangle-square should measure 2" square, including the seam allowances. Repeat to make a total of 432 triangle-squares.

Diagram 1

2. Referring to Diagram 2 for placement, sew together nine triangle-squares in three horizontal rows. Press the seam allowances in each row in one direction, alternating the direction with each row. Then join the rows to make a triangle unit. Press the seam allowances away from the center row. The pieced unit should measure 5" square, including the seam allowances. Repeat to make a total of 48 triangle units.

Diagram 2

Rectangle Units

1. Aligning long edges, sew two muslin 2×42" strips to an orange print 2×42" strip to make a strip set (see Diagram 3). Press the seam allowances toward the orange print strip. Repeat to make a total of six strip sets.

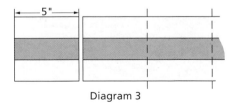

Diagram 3

2. Cut the strip sets into 5"-wide segments for a total of 48 rectangle units.

Center Units

1. Referring to Diagram 4, sew a solid orange $1\frac{1}{4}×3\frac{1}{2}$" rectangle to opposite edges of a muslin $3\frac{1}{2}$" square. Press the seam allowances toward the orange rectangles.

Diagram 4

2. Join a solid orange $1\frac{1}{4}×5$" rectangle to the remaining edges of the muslin $3\frac{1}{2}$" square to make a center unit. Press the seam allowances toward the orange rectangles. The pieced center unit should measure 5" square, including the seam allowances. Repeat to make a total of 12 center units.

ASSEMBLE THE BLOCKS

1. Referring to Diagram 5 for placement, lay out four triangle units, four rectangle units, and one center unit in three horizontal rows. Sew together the pieces in each row. Press the seam allowances toward the rectangle units. Then join the rows to make a geometric puzzle block. The finished block should measure 14" square, including the seam allowances.

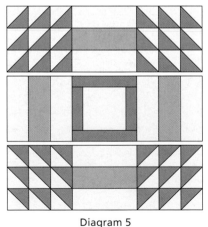

Diagram 5

2. Repeat to make a total of 12 blocks.

ASSEMBLE THE QUILT CENTER

1. Referring to the photograph *above* for placement, lay out the 12 pieced blocks, the six muslin 14" setting squares, the 10 side setting triangles, and the four corner triangles in diagonal rows.

2. Sew together the pieces in each diagonal row, except for the corner triangles. Press the seam allowances toward the setting squares and setting triangles. Join the rows. Press the seam allowances in one direction.

3. Add the corner triangles to complete the quilt center. The pieced quilt center should measure 57⅞×77", including the seam allowances.

ADD THE BORDERS

1. Cut and piece the orange print 1½×42" strips to make the following:
- 2—1½×77" inner border strips
- 2—1½×57⅞" inner border strips

2. Cut and piece the muslin 3×42" strips to make the following:
- 2—3×77" outer border strips
- 2—3×57⅞" outer border strips

3. Join one orange print 1½×77" inner border strip and one muslin 3×77" outer border strip along a pair of long edges to make a side border unit. Press the seam allowance toward the orange print strip. Repeat to make a second side border unit.

4. Join the side border units to the side edges of the quilt center. Press the seam allowances toward the border unit.

5. Sew together one orange print 1½×57⅞" inner border strip and one muslin 3×57⅞"

outer border strip along long edges. Press the seam allowance toward the orange print strip. Sew a muslin 4" square to each end of the pieced strip to make the top border unit. Join the top border to the top edge of the pieced quilt center. Press the seam allowance toward the pieced border.

6. Repeat Step 5 to make the bottom border unit. Join it to the bottom edge of the pieced quilt center to complete the quilt top.

COMPLETE THE QUILT

1. Layer the quilt top, batting, and backing according to the instructions in Quilter's Schoolhouse, which begins on *page 131*.

2. Quilt as desired. Quilter Dawn Cavanaugh machine-quilted the muslin setting squares and triangles and the centers of the puzzle blocks with a feather motif.

3. Use the solid orange 2½×42" strips to bind the quilt according to the instructions in Quilter's Schoolhouse.

COLOR OPTION

Bright batiks caught quilt tester Laura Boehnke's eye as colorful possibilities for a single block of "Geometric Puzzle." With offsetting triangles in fuchsia and two borders in green, the block becomes a small wall hanging.

Posy Patch

We borrowed blooms from Jean Ray Laury's appliqué headboard (see photograph on page 118) in a 1964 issue of Better Homes and Gardens *magazine to make a cheery accent pillow.*

2. Following the manufacturer's instructions, press the fusible web shapes onto the backs of the designated fabrics; let cool. Cut out the fabric shapes on the drawn lines. Peel off the paper backings.

From tan batik, cut:
- 1—14×18" rectangle for appliqué foundation
- 1—13×17" rectangle for pillow backing

From assorted green batiks, cut:
- 1 *each* of patterns A, B, C, D, E, F, L, and M
- 3 of Pattern H
- 2 of Pattern I
- 3 of Pattern K

From assorted yellow, red, orange, pink, peach, gold, and blue batiks, cut:
- 1 *each* of patterns G, G reversed, I, J, L, N, O, P, Q, and R
- 5 of Pattern H

APPLIQUÉ THE PILLOW TOP

1. Referring to the photograph on *page 117* and the Appliqué Placement Diagram *below*, position the prepared flower and leaf appliqué pieces on the tan batik 14×18" rectangle. When you're pleased with the arrangement, fuse them in place.

MATERIALS
½ yard of tan batik for appliqué foundation and pillow backing
Scraps of assorted green batiks for leaf and stem appliqués
Scraps of yellow, red, orange, pink, peach, gold, and blue batiks for leaf, flower, and butterfly appliqués
12×16" pillow form
¼ yard of lightweight fusible web
Machine embroidery thread in assorted colors

Finished pillow: 12×16"

Quantities specified for 44/45"-wide 100% cotton fabrics. Sew with right sides together unless otherwise stated.

CUT THE FABRICS
To make the best use of your fabrics, cut the pieces in the order that follows. The patterns are on *page 137*.

To use fusible web for appliqué, as was done in this project, complete the following steps.

1. Lay the fusible web, paper side up, over the patterns. Use a pencil to trace each pattern the specified number of times, leaving ½" between tracings. Cut out the pieces roughly ¼" outside of the traced lines.

Appliqué Placement Diagram

2. Use matching or contrasting machine embroidery thread to appliqué the pieces to the foundation. Quiltmaker Randall Parkin used a dense satin stitch to stitch the butterfly body and antennae, and to stitch the wing, flower, and leaf shapes in place.

3. Centering the appliquéd design, trim the appliquéd pillow top to measure 13×17", including the seam allowances.

COMPLETE THE PILLOW

1. Stitch together the appliquéd pillow top and the tan batik pillow backing, using a ½" seam allowance and leaving a 5" to 6" opening at the bottom (see Diagram 1).

2. To shape the corners, match seams on adjacent sides of pillow top, creating a flattened triangle (see Diagram 2). Measure and mark a dot 2½" from the point of the corner on the two folded edges. Draw a line between the dots, then stitch across the drawn line. Repeat at each corner; press. Turn the pillow right side out.

3. Insert the pillow form through the opening. Whipstitch the opening closed.

COLOR OPTION

Instead of batiks, quilt tester Laura Boehnke selected assorted print scraps to create the posies that circle a round tablecloth, shown *above*.

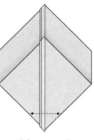

Diagram 1   Diagram 2

JEAN RAY LAURY'S NEW-STYLE QUILTS

Referred to as a leader in 20th-century contemporary quilt design, Jean Ray Laury was first recognized when she created a quilt for a graduate art class at Stanford University. For "Tom's Quilt," Jean appliquéd blocks of all the toys and tools that interested her 4-year-old son—a kite, train, building blocks, eggbeater, alarm clock, toothpaste tube and toothbrush, a fork, and spoon. Two years later, she entered the quilt in a contest at the Eastern States Exposition in Springfield, Massachusetts. The quilt did not win a prize, but a needlework editor for *House Beautiful* magazine noticed Jean's work and invited the artist to write articles for the magazine. This national exposure brought Jean requests to lecture, give workshops, and design for women's magazines. *Better Homes and Gardens* magazine featured her designs for crafts projects in patchwork, appliqué, and creative stitchery in the 1960s. In 1982, Jean was inducted into the Quilters Hall of Fame "as a pioneer quilt and textile designer." In 1999, one of her quilts was chosen among the top 100 quilts of the 20th century.

Star-Spangled Beauty

More than 25 years have passed since this quilt—created for America's Bicentennial—graced the cover of Better Homes and Gardens. *The color scheme remains the same, though our current fabrics carry star and flag motifs.*

MATERIALS FOR QUILT

5¼ yards of red print for blocks, sashing, outer border, and binding
1½ yards of blue print for blocks
4½ yards of solid white for blocks, sashing, and inner border
⅜ yard of patriotic print for sashing squares
7½ yards of backing fabric
89×103" of quilt batting

Finished quilt top: 82½×97"
Finished block: 12" square

Quantities specified for 44/45"-wide, 100% cotton fabrics. All measurements include a ¼" seam allowance. Sew with right sides together unless otherwise stated.

CUT THE FABRICS

To make the best use of your fabrics, cut the pieces in the order that follows. The patterns are on *page 138*. To make templates for the patterns, follow the instructions in Quilter's Schoolhouse, which begins on *page 131*.

The border strips are cut the length of the fabric (parallel to the selvage). The listings include mathematically correct border lengths. You may wish to cut your strips longer than specified to allow for possible sewing differences.

From red print, cut:
• 2—2½×93½" outer border strips
• 2—2½×83" outer border strips
• 9—2½×42" binding strips
• 142—1¼×12½" sashing strips
• 120 of Pattern A
From blue print, cut:
• 120 of Pattern A reversed

From solid white, cut:
- 2—2¼×90" inner border strips
- 2—2¼×79" inner border strips
- 71—1½×12½" sashing strips
- 120—4" squares *or* 120 of Pattern C
- 120 of Pattern B

From patriotic print, cut:
- 42—3" sashing squares

ASSEMBLE THE STAR BLOCKS

1. For one Star block you'll need four red print Pattern A diamonds, four blue print Pattern A reversed diamonds, four white B triangles, and four white C squares.

2. Pin together one red A and one blue A reversed diamond. Carefully align the matching points (see Diagram 1). A matching point is where the seam should begin or end, ¼" from the end of each piece, so you do not sew into a seam allowance needed for a future piece. Sew together diamonds, stopping precisely at the matching points, to make a diamond pair. Repeat to make a total of four diamond pairs.

Diagram 1

3. With right sides together, pin one piece of the diamond pair to one short side of the B triangle. (See Diagram 2 for placement of the B triangle and diamond pair.)

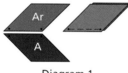

Diagram 2   Diagram 3

4. Match the seam's matching points, pushing a pin through both fabric layers to check the alignment. Machine-stitch the seam, backstitching to secure ends and stopping at the matching points (see Diagram 3). Do not stitch into the ¼" seam allowances. Remove the unit from the sewing machine. Bring the adjacent edge of the angled unit up and align it with the other short edge of the triangle.

Insert a pin in each corner to align matching points, then pin the remainder of the seam. Machine-stitch between matching points as before. Press seam allowances of the set-in piece away from it. Repeat to make a total of four double-diamond subunits.

5. Sew together two of the double-diamond subunits as shown in Diagram 4 to form one partial-star unit. Align the matching points as before and do not sew into the ¼" seam allowances at each end. Attach a white square to one of the partial-star units, following the directions for attaching the triangles. Repeat with the remaining two double-diamond subunits. Sew together the two partial-star units (see Diagram 5), making sure not to sew into the ¼" seam allowance.

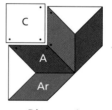

Diagram 4

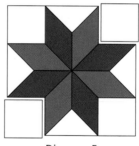

Diagram 5

6. Set in the remaining two white C squares to complete a Star block. The pieced Star block should measure 12½" square, including the seam allowances.

7. Repeat steps 2 through 6 to make a total of 30 Star blocks.

ASSEMBLE THE STRIPED SASHING STRIPS

1. For each striped sashing strip, you'll need two red print 1¼×12½" sashing strips and one solid white 1½×12½" sashing strip.

THE STARS BEHIND THE QUILT

In celebration of America's 200th birthday, *Better Homes and Gardens* featured a star-studded quilt on the cover of the February 1976 issue. Mrs. Arthur "Willie" Woodburn of Texas, who pieced the quilt, and Mabel Metcalf of Oklahoma, *right*, who quilted it, were two of seven quilters featured in the magazine as the "Southwest Quilters." Having grown up in the early part of the 20th century, the women and their quilting memories created a charming American story rooted in heritage and love. They spoke of times when, as Willie explained, "everything was precious." As a young girl, she would pick up fabric pieces that her mother dropped on the floor and stash them away in her scrap box. "They taught us not to waste," said a featured quilter from New Mexico. While some of the women quilted in order to pay for food and keep warm, others quilted to keep memories alive. "I quilted for all my babies and grandbabies," said Mabel. "Keeps me busy, quiltin' for all of 'em."

(For information on how the Southwest Quilters inspired a Broadway play, see *page 80*.)

2. Referring to Diagram 6, join a red print strip to each long side of the solid white strip. Press the seam allowances toward the red print strips. The striped sashing strip should measure 3×12½", including the seam allowances.

Diagram 6

3. Repeat Step 2 to make a total of 71 striped sashing strips.

ASSEMBLE THE QUILT CENTER

1. Referring to the photograph on *page 123,* lay out the 30 Star blocks, the 71 striped sashing strips, and the forty-two 3" patriotic print sashing squares in 13 horizontal rows.

2. Sew together the pieces in each row. Press the seam allowances in one direction, alternating the direction with each row. Join the rows to make the quilt center. Press the seam allowances in one direction. The pieced quilt center should measure 75½×90", including the seam allowances.

ADD THE BORDERS

1. Sew the solid white 2¼×90" inner border strips to the side edges of the pieced quilt center. Then add the solid white 2¼×79" inner border strips to the top and bottom edges of the pieced quilt center. Press all seam allowances toward the white border.

2. Join the red print 2½×93½" outer border strips to the side edges of the quilt center. Then add the red print 2½×83" outer border strips to the top and bottom edges of the pieced quilt center to complete the quilt top. Press all seam allowances toward the red print border.

COMPLETE THE QUILT

1. Layer the quilt top, batting, and backing according to the instructions in Quilter's Schoolhouse, which begins on *page 131.*

2. Quilt as desired. Quiltmaker Jill Reber machine-stitched through the center of each diamond in each Star block and made ovals in the middle of each sashing unit.

3. Use the red print 2½×42" strips to bind the quilt according to the instructions in Quilter's Schoolhouse.

COLOR OPTION

ountry prints in earth tones from the scrap basket were quilt tester Laura Boehnke's choice for creating a totally different look with the block. Even so, she found several fabrics printed with stars to carry out the star theme. Four of the large blocks with sashing and a single border create a wall hanging.

MATERIALS FOR ONE PILLOW SHAM

¼ yard of red print for block and border
1½ yards of blue print for block, border, and pillow sham back
¼ yard of solid white for block and border
¾ yard of muslin for lining
26×31" of quilt batting

Finished size: Fits one standard bed pillow

CUT THE FABRICS

From red print, cut:
• 2—2½×16½" inner border strips
• 2—2½×12½" inner border strips
• 4 of Pattern A

From blue print, cut:
• 2—21×32" rectangles for pillow sham back
• 2—4½×20½" outer border strips
• 2—2×28½" outer border strips
• 4 of Pattern A reversed

From solid white, cut:
• 2—2½×20½" middle border strips
• 2—2½×16½" middle border strips
• 4 of Pattern B
• 4—4" squares *or* 4 of Pattern C

ASSEMBLE THE PILLOW TOP

1. Piece one Star block as for quilt. See Assemble the Star Blocks on *page 122*.

2. Referring to the Pillow Sham Assembly Diagram, sew the red 2½×12½" inner border strips to opposite edges of the pieced Star block. Sew the red 2½×16½" inner border strips to the remaining edges of the block. Press the seam allowances toward the red border.

3. Sew the solid white 2½×16½" middle border strips to opposite edges of the block. Sew the

solid white 2½×20½" middle border strips to the remaining edges of the block. Press the seam allowances toward the red border.

4. Sew the blue print 4½×20½" outer border strips to opposite edges of the block. Sew the blue print 2×28½" outer border strips to the remaining edges of the block to complete the pillow sham top. Press the seam allowances toward the blue border.

5. Layer the pillow sham top, batting, and lining according to the instructions in Quilter's Schoolhouse, which begins on *page 131*. Quilt as desired. Quiltmaker Jill Reber machine-quilted through the center of each diamond of the Star block and outline-quilted the borders of the pillow sham.

6. Centering the Star block, trim the quilted pillow sham top to measure 21×27", including the seam allowances.

ASSEMBLE THE PILLOW SHAM

1. With wrong sides together, fold the two blue print 21×32" rectangles in half to form two 21×16" double-thick pillow sham back pieces.

2. Overlap the two folded edges by about 4". Using a ½" seam allowance, stitch the pieces along the long edges and across the folds to create a single pillow sham back.

3. With right sides together, layer and pin the edges of the pillow sham top and back together; join. Trim the pillow sham back and corner seam allowances as needed. Turn the sham right side out. Insert the pillow.

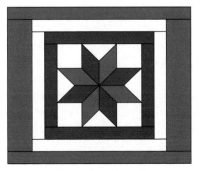

Pillow Sham Assembly Diagram

Happy Days

Peggy Waltman, whose works have appeared in American Patchwork & Quilting *magazine, created a wall hanging that features traditional appliqué and piecing, contemporary fabrics, and machine quilting.*

MATERIALS

⅝ yard of solid white for blocks and appliqué foundations
⅜ yard of blue polka dot for blocks and flower and scallop appliqués
⅛ yard of blue print for blocks and flower appliqués
1¼ yards of red print for blocks, flower appliqués, and border
⅛ yard of red check for blocks
⅛ yard *each* of yellow check and yellow print for blocks and flower appliqués
Scraps of light blue and dark blue Ultrasuede for berry appliqués
Scraps of assorted green prints for leaf appliqués
⅝ yard of red-and-white print for corner triangles
⅜ yard of green print for scallop appliqués
¼ yard of dark yellow print for border
⅝ yard of red tone-on-tone plaid for binding
48" square of quilt batting
2⅝ yards of backing fabric
Green perle cotton thread

Finished quilt top: 41½" square
Finished block: 8" square

Quantities specified for 44/45"-wide 100% cotton fabrics. All measurements include a ¼" seam allowance.
Sew with right sides together unless otherwise stated.

CUT THE FABRICS

To make the best use of your fabrics, cut the pieces in the order that follows.

The patterns are on *page 143*. To make templates of the patterns, follow the instructions in Quilter's Schoolhouse, which begins on *page 131*. If using traditional appliqué, as was done in this project, remember to add a ³⁄₁₆" seam allowance when cutting out appliqué pieces from cotton fabrics, except for the long, straight edges on patterns G and H. Pieces cut from Ultrasuede (Pattern E) do not need seam allowances because the raw edges will not ravel.

The border strips are cut the length of the fabric (parallel to the selvage) and are cut longer than necessary to allow for mitering the corners.

From solid white, cut:
• 4—8½" squares for appliqué foundations
• 10—2⅞" squares
• 20—2⅞" squares, cutting each in half diagonally for a total of 40 large triangles
• 10—2⅝" squares, cutting each in half diagonally for a total of 20 small triangles
From blue polka dot, cut:
• 6—2⅞" squares
• 4 *each* of patterns C and G
From blue print, cut:
• 4—2⅞" squares
• 4 of Pattern C

From red print, cut:
- 4—1½×44" strips for border
- 4—1¼×44" strips for border
- 4—2⅞" squares
- 8—1⅝" squares
- 4 of Pattern A

From red check, cut:
- 1—2⅞" square
- 12—1⅝" squares

From yellow check, cut:
- 8—1⅝×3⅞" rectangles

From yellow print, cut:
- 12—1⅝×3⅞" rectangles
- 8 *each* of patterns B and B reversed

From light and dark blue Ultrasuede scraps, cut:
- 36 of Pattern E

From assorted green print scraps, cut:
- 16 of Pattern D
- 12 of Pattern F

From red-and-white print, cut:
- 2—19½" squares, cutting each in half diagonally for a total of 4 corner triangles

From green print, cut:
- 4 of Pattern H

From dark yellow print, cut:
- 5—1×42" strips for border

From red tone-on-tone plaid, cut:
- 1—22" square, cutting it into enough 2½"-wide bias strips to total 170" in length for binding (For specific instructions on cutting bias strips, see Quilter's Schoolhouse, which begins on *page 131*.)

ASSEMBLE THE TRIANGLE UNITS

1. Use a quilting pencil to mark a diagonal line on the wrong side of each of the blue polka-dot and blue print 2⅞" squares. (To prevent your fabric from stretching as you draw the lines, place 220-grit sandpaper under the squares.)

2. Layer a marked blue polka-dot or blue print 2⅞" square atop a solid white 2⅞" square. Referring to Diagram 1, sew the pair together with two seams, stitching ¼" on each side of the drawn line.

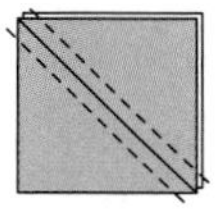

Diagram 1

3. Cut on the drawn line (see Diagram 2) and press the pieced units open, pressing

Diagram 2

the seam allowances toward the blue triangles to make two triangle-squares (see Diagram 3). Repeat steps 2 and 3 to make a total of 20 triangle-squares.

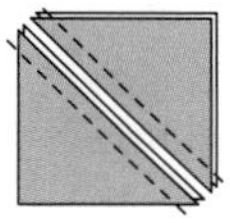

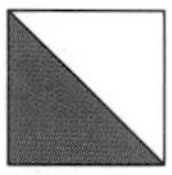

Diagram 3

4. Referring to Diagram 4, join two solid white large triangles to the blue edges of a triangle-square to make a triangle unit. Press the seam allowances toward the white triangles. Repeat to make a total of 20 triangle units.

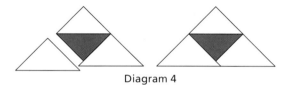

Diagram 4

ASSEMBLE THE SQUARE UNITS

1. Sew two solid white small triangles to opposite side edges of a red print or check 2⅞" square (see Diagram 5). Press the seam allowances toward the triangles. Sew two more solid white small triangles to the remaining raw edges of the red square to make a center subunit (see Diagram 6). Press the seam allowances toward the white triangles.

Diagram 5   Diagram 6

2. Sew two matching yellow check or yellow print 1⅝×3⅞" rectangles to opposite edges of the center subunit (see Diagram 7). Press the seam allowances toward the yellow rectangles.

3. Sew matching red print or red check 1⅝" squares to short edges of two matching yellow check or yellow print 1⅝×3⅞"

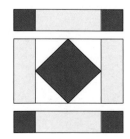

Diagram 7

rectangles to make two pieced rectangle subunits (see Diagram 7). Press the seam allowances toward the yellow rectangles.

4. Sew the pieced rectangle subunits to the remaining edges of the center subunit to make a square unit. Press the seam allowances toward the rectangle subunits.

5. Repeat steps 1 through 4 to make a total of five square units.

ASSEMBLE THE BLOCKS

1. Sew a triangle unit to opposite edges of a square unit (see Diagram 8). Press the seam allowances toward the square unit.

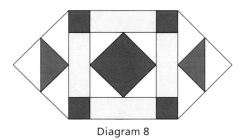

Diagram 8

2. Sew a triangle unit to the remaining raw edges of the square unit to make a pieced block (see Diagram 9). Press the seam allowances toward the square unit. The pieced block should measure 8½" square, including the seam allowances.

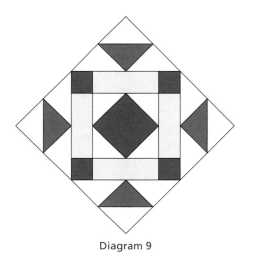

Diagram 9

3. Repeat steps 1 and 2 to make a total of five pieced blocks.

ASSEMBLE THE APPLIQUÉ UNITS

1. Referring to Diagram 10 and the Full-Size Pattern Placement Diagram on *page 143,* embroider stems on each red print A piece using a stem stitch and one strand of green perle cotton thread.

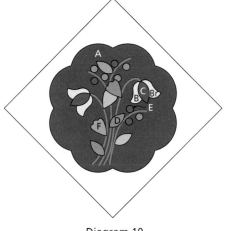

Diagram 10

To stem-stitch, pull your needle up at A (see diagram *right*). Insert your needle back into the fabric at B, about ⅜" away from A. Holding the thread out of the way, bring your needle back up at C and pull the thread through so it lies flat against the fabric. The distances between points A, B, and C should be equal. Pull with equal tautness after each stitch. Continue in the same manner.

Stem Stitch

2. Arrange the leaf, flower, and berry appliqué pieces on each embroidered A piece; baste in place. Using small slip stitches and threads that match the fabrics, appliqué the pieces in place.

3. Fold each solid white 8½" square in half diagonally in both directions and lightly finger-press to form placement lines. Fold each appliquéd unit in half horizontally and vertically and lightly finger-press.

4. Align the center of an appliquéd unit with the center of a foundation square. Rotate the appliquéd unit until it is on point in the center of the foundation square; baste in place. Appliqué the appliquéd unit to the foundation square using red thread to make an appliquéd block.

5. Repeat step 4 to make four appliquéd blocks.

ASSEMBLE THE QUILT CENTER
1. Referring to the Quilt Assembly Diagram for placement, lay out the appliquéd blocks and pieced blocks in three diagonal rows. Sew together the blocks in each row. Press the seam allowances toward the appliquéd blocks. Then join the rows to make the center unit. The center unit should measure 24½" square, including the seam allowances.

2. Center and align the straight edges of a red-and-white print corner triangle and a blue polka-dot G strip. Baste in place. Turning under the strip's scalloped edge and using blue thread, appliqué the strip to the triangle.

3. Center and align the straight edges of a green print H strip and the appliquéd blue strip. Baste in place. Turning under the green strip's scalloped edge and using green thread, appliqué the green strip to the blue strip to make a corner unit.

4. Repeat steps 2 and 3 to make a total of four corner units.

5. Referring to the Quilt Assembly Diagram, sew two corner units to opposite edges of the center unit. Press the seam allowances toward the corner units. Sew the remaining corner units to the remaining raw edges of the block unit to complete the quilt center. Press the seam allowances toward the corner units. The pieced quilt center should measure 37½" square, including the seam allowances.

ADD THE BORDERS
1. Cut and piece the dark yellow print 1×42" strips to make the following:
• 4—1×44" border strips

2. Aligning long edges, sew one red print 1¼×44" strip and one red print 1½×44" strip to each dark yellow border strip to make a

Quilt Assembly Diagram

pieced border unit (see Diagram 11). Press the seam allowances toward the red strips. Repeat to make a total of four pieced border units.

Diagram 11

3. Sew the pieced border units to the edges of the pieced quilt center with the narrowest red print strip toward the quilt center, mitering the corners to complete the quilt top. For instructions on mitering, see Quilter's Schoolhouse, which begins on *page 131.*

COMPLETE THE QUILT
1. Layer the quilt top, batting, and backing according to the instructions in Quilter's Schoolhouse.

2. Quilt as desired. Quilter Laurel Barrus machine-quilted around the blocks in an echo and stipple pattern.

3. Use the red tone-on-tone plaid 2½"-wide bias strips to bind the quilt according to the instructions in Quilter's Schoolhouse.

Refer to your personal "classroom" of tools, tips, and techniques whenever you need information on cutting, piecing, quilting, or finishing your projects.

TOOLS

Before you begin any quilting project, collect the tools and materials you'll need in one easy-to-access place. Below is a list of general supplies.

CUTTING

• **Acrylic ruler:** For making perfectly straight cuts with a rotary cutter, choose a ruler of thick, clear plastic. Many sizes are available. A 6×24" ruler marked in ¼" increments with 30°, 45°, and 60° angles is a good first purchase.

• **Rotary cutter and mat:** These tools have revolutionized quilting because a rotary cutter's round blade cuts strips, squares, triangles, and diamonds more quickly, efficiently, and accurately than scissors. A rotary cutter should always be used with a mat designed specifically for it. In addition to protecting the table, the mat helps keep the fabric from shifting while you cut.

• **Scissors:** You'll need one pair for fabric and another for paper and plastic.

• **Pencils and other marking tools:** Marks made with special fabric markers are easier to remove after sewing and quilting.

• **Template plastic:** This slightly frosted plastic comes in sheets about ⅛" thick.

PIECING

• **Iron and ironing board:** Pressing the seams ensures accurate piecing.

• **Sewing machine:** Any machine with well-adjusted tension will produce pucker-free patchwork seams.

• **Thread:** Use 100% cotton thread in your machine.

APPLIQUÉ

• **Fusible web:** Instead of using a traditional basting method, secure cutout shapes to the background of an appliqué block with lightweight iron-on adhesive.

• **Needles:** For hand appliqué, most quilters like fine quilting needles.

HAND QUILTING

• **Frame or hoop:** You'll get smaller, more even stitches if you stretch your quilt as you stitch. A frame supports the quilt's weight, ensures even tension, and frees both your hands for stitching. However, once set up, it cannot be disassembled until the quilting is complete. Hoops are more portable and less expensive. Quilting hoops are deeper than embroidery hoops to accommodate the thickness of quilt layers.

• **Needles:** A "between" or quilting needle is short with a small eye. Common sizes are 8, 9, and 10; size 8 is best for beginners.

• **Thread:** Quilting thread, including the preferred 100% cotton variety, is stronger than sewing thread.

• **Thimble:** This finger cover relieves the pressure required to push a needle through several layers of fabric and batting.

MACHINE QUILTING

• **Darning foot:** You may find this sewing machine attachment, also called a hopper foot, in your machine's accessory kit. If not, have the model and brand of your machine available when you go to purchase one. It is used for free-motion stitching.

• **Safety pins:** They hold the layers together during quilting.

• **Table or other large work surface that's level with your machine bed:** Your quilt will need the support.

• **Thread:** Use 100% cotton quilting thread, cotton-wrapped polyester quilting thread, or very fine nylon monofilament thread.

• **Walking foot:** This sewing-machine accessory helps keep long, straight quilting lines smooth and pucker-free.

CHOOSE YOUR FABRICS

The best fabric for quiltmaking is 100% cotton because it minimizes seam distortion, presses crisply, and is easy to quilt. Our instructions specify quantities for 44/45"-wide fabrics unless otherwise noted. Our projects call for a little extra yardage to allow for minor errors and slight shrinkage.

PREPARE YOUR FABRICS

Prewashing fabric offers quilters certainty as its main advantage. Today's fabrics resist bleeding and shrinking, but some of both can occur in some fabrics—an unpleasant prospect once you've assembled the quilt. Some quilters find prewashed fabric easier to quilt. If you choose to prewash your fabric, press it well before cutting.

Other quilters prefer the crispness of unwashed fabric for machine piecing. And, if you use fabrics with the same fiber content throughout the quilt, any shrinkage that occurs in its first washing should be uniform. Some quilters find this small amount of shrinkage desirable, since it gives the quilt a slightly puckered, antique look.

We recommend you prewash a scrap of each fabric to test it for shrinkage and bleeding. If you choose to prewash a fabric, unfold it to a single layer. Wash it in warm water to allow the fabric to shrink and/or bleed. If the fabric bleeds, rinse it until the water runs clear. Don't use any fabric in your quilt if it hasn't stopped bleeding. Hang fabric to dry, or tumble it in the dryer until slightly damp.

CUT BIAS STRIPS

Strips for curved appliqué pattern pieces and for binding curved edges should be cut on the bias (diagonally across the grain of a woven fabric), which runs at a 45° angle to the selvage and has the most stretch.

To cut bias strips, begin with a fabric square or rectangle; use a large acrylic ruler to square up the left edge. Make a cut at a 45° angle to the left edge (see Bias Strips Diagram). Handle the diagonal edges carefully to avoid distorting the bias. To cut a strip, measure the desired width from the 45° cut edge; cut parallel to the 45° edge. Cut enough strips to total the length needed.

Bias Strips Diagram

MAKE COVERED CORDING

Covered cording is made by sewing a bias-cut fabric strip around a length of cording. The width of the bias strip will vary depending on the diameter of your cording. Refer to the specific project instructions for those measurements. Regardless, the method used to cover the cording is the same.

With the wrong side inside, fold under 1½" at one end of the bias strip. With the wrong side inside, fold the strip in half lengthwise to make the cording cover. Insert the cording next to the folded edge, placing a cording end 1" from the cording cover's folded end. Using a machine cording foot, sew through both fabric layers right next to the cording (see Diagram 1).

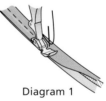

Diagram 1

When attaching the cording to your project, begin stitching 1½" from the covered cording's folded end. Round the corners slightly, making sure the corner curves match. As you stitch each corner, gently ease the covered cording into place (see Diagram 2).

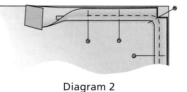

Diagram 2

After going around the entire edge of the project, cut the end of the cording so that it will fit snugly into the folded opening at the beginning (see Diagram 3). The ends of the cording should abut inside the covering. Stitch the ends in place to secure (see Diagram 4).

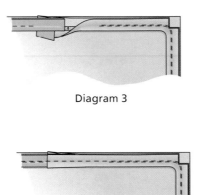

Diagram 3

Diagram 4

MAKE THE TEMPLATES

A template is a pattern made from extra-sturdy material so you can trace around it many times without wearing away the edges. Acrylic templates for many common shapes are available at quilt shops. You can also make your own by duplicating printed patterns on plastic.

To make permanent templates, we recommend using easy-to-cut template plastic, available at crafts supply stores. This material lasts indefinitely, and its transparency allows you to trace the pattern directly onto its surface.

To make a template, lay the plastic over a printed pattern. Trace the pattern onto the plastic using a ruler and a permanent marker. This will ensure straight lines, accurate corners, and permanency.

For hand piecing and appliqué, make templates the exact size of the finished pieces, without seam allowances, by tracing the patterns' dashed lines.

For machine piecing, make templates with the seam allowances included.

For easy reference, mark each template with its letter designation, grain line if noted, and block name. Verify the template's size by placing it over the printed pattern. Templates must be accurate or the error, however small, will compound many times as you assemble a quilt. To check the accuracy of your templates,

make a test block before cutting the fabric pieces for an entire quilt.

TRACE THE TEMPLATES

To mark on fabric, use a pencil, white dressmaker's pencil, chalk, or a special fabric marker that makes a thin, accurate line. Do not use a ballpoint or ink pen; it may bleed if washed. Test all marking tools on a fabric scrap before using them.

To trace pieces that will be used for hand piecing or appliqué, place templates facedown on the wrong side of the fabric and trace; position the templates at least ½" apart (see Diagram 5). The lines drawn on the fabric are the sewing lines. Mark cutting lines ¼" away from the sewing lines or estimate the distance by eye when cutting out the pieces. For hand piecing, add a ¼" seam allowance; for hand appliqué, add a ³⁄₁₆" seam allowance.

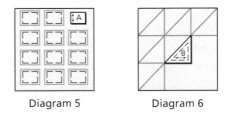

Diagram 5   Diagram 6

Templates used to make pieces for machine piecing have seam allowances included so you can use common lines for efficient cutting. Place templates facedown on the wrong side of the fabric and trace; do not leave spaces between templates (see Diagram 6). Using sharp scissors or a rotary cutter and ruler, cut precisely on the drawn (cutting) lines.

PLAN FOR CUTTING

Project instructions list pieces in the order they should be cut to make the best use of your fabrics. Always consider the fabric grain before cutting. The arrow on a pattern piece indicates which direction the fabric grain should run. One or more straight sides of the pattern piece should follow the fabric's lengthwise or crosswise grain.

The lengthwise grain, parallel to the selvage (the tightly finished edge), has the least amount of stretch. Crosswise grain, perpendicular to the selvage, has a little more give. The edge of any pattern piece that will be on the outside of a block or quilt should always be cut on the lengthwise grain. (Do not use the selvage of a woven fabric in a quilt. When washed, it may shrink more than the rest of the fabric.)

In projects larger than 42" in length or width, we specify that the border strips be cut the width (crosswise grain) of the fabric and pieced to use the least amount of fabric. If you'd prefer to cut the border strips on the lengthwise grain and not piece them, you'll need to refigure the yardage.

CREATE MITERED BORDERS

To add a border with mitered corners, first pin a border strip to a quilt top edge, matching the center of the strip and the center of the quilt top edge. Sew together, beginning and ending the seam ¼" from the quilt-top corners (see Diagram 7). Allow excess border fabric to extend beyond the edges. Repeat with remaining border strips. Press the seam allowances toward the border strips.

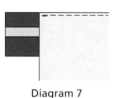

Diagram 7

At one corner lap one border strip over the other (see Diagram 8). Align the edge of a 90° right triangle with the raw edge of the top strip so the long edge of the triangle intersects the border seam in the corner. With a pencil, draw along the edge of the triangle from the seam out to the raw edge. Place the bottom border strip on top and repeat the marking process.

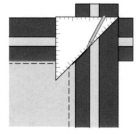

Diagram 8

With the right sides together, match the marked seam lines and pin (see Diagram 9).

Beginning with a backstitch at the quilt top edge, sew together the strips, stitching exactly on the marked lines. Check the right side to see that the corner lies flat. Trim the excess fabric, leaving a ¼" seam allowance. Press the seam open. Mark and sew the remaining corners in the same manner.

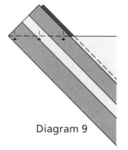

Diagram 9

COMPLETE THE QUILT

Cut and piece the backing fabric to measure at least 3" bigger on all sides than the quilt top. Press all seam allowances open. With wrong sides together, layer the quilt top and backing fabric with the batting in between; baste. Quilt as desired.

The binding for most quilts is cut on the straight grain of the fabric. If your quilt has curved edges, cut the strips on the bias (see *page 132*). The cutting instructions for projects in this book specify the number of binding strips or a total length needed to finish the quilt. The instructions also specify enough width for a French-fold, or double-layer, binding because it's easier to apply and adds durability.

Join the strips with diagonal seams (see Diagram 10) to make one continuous binding strip. Trim the excess fabric, leaving ¼" seam allowances. Press the seam allowances open. With the wrong side inside, fold under 1" at one end of the binding strip (see Diagram 11); press. Fold the strip in half lengthwise (see Diagram 12); press.

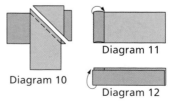

Diagram 10

Diagram 11

Diagram 12

Beginning in the center of one side of the quilt, place the binding strip against the right side of the quilt top, aligning the binding strip's raw edges with the quilt top's raw edge (see Diagram 13). Beginning 1½" from the folded edge, sew through all layers, stopping ¼" from the corner. Backstitch; clip the threads. Remove the quilt from under the sewing-machine presser foot.

Fold the binding strip upward (see Diagram 14), creating a diagonal fold, and finger-press.

Holding the diagonal fold in place with your finger, bring the binding strip down in line with the next edge, making a horizontal fold that aligns with the quilt edge (see Diagram 15).

Start sewing again at the quilt edge, stitching through all layers. Sew around the quilt, turning each corner in the same manner.

When you return to the starting point, encase the binding strip raw edge inside the folded end (see Diagram 16). Finish sewing to the starting point (see Diagram 17). Trim the batting and backing fabric even with the quilt top edges.

Turn the binding over the quilt edge. Hand-stitch the binding to the backing fabric, making sure to cover any machine stitching.

To make mitered corners on the back, hand-stitch up to a corner; fold a miter in the binding. Take a stitch or two in the fold to secure it. Then stitch the binding in place up to the next corner. Finish each corner in the same manner.

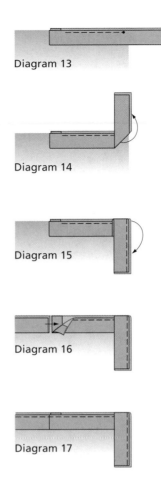

Diagram 13

Diagram 14

Diagram 15

Diagram 16

Diagram 17

patterns

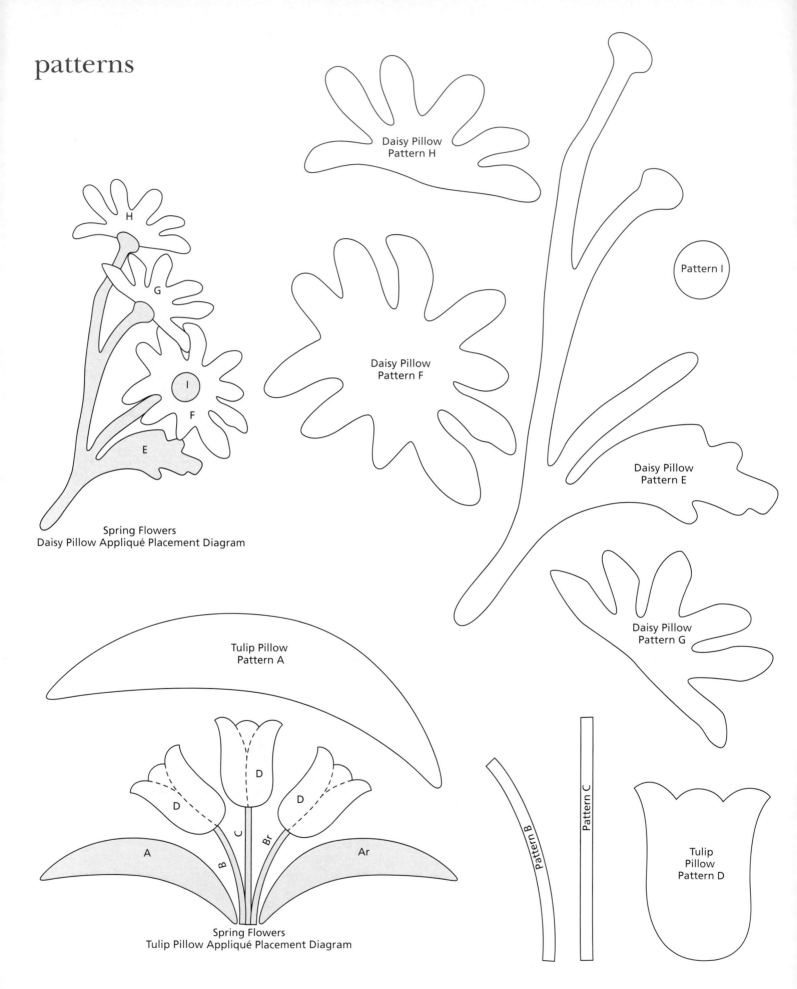

Daisy Pillow
Pattern H

Pattern I

Daisy Pillow
Pattern F

Daisy Pillow
Pattern E

H

G

I

F

E

Spring Flowers
Daisy Pillow Appliqué Placement Diagram

Daisy Pillow
Pattern G

Tulip Pillow
Pattern A

D

D

D

A

B

C

Br

Ar

Pattern B

Pattern C

Tulip
Pillow
Pattern D

Spring Flowers
Tulip Pillow Appliqué Placement Diagram

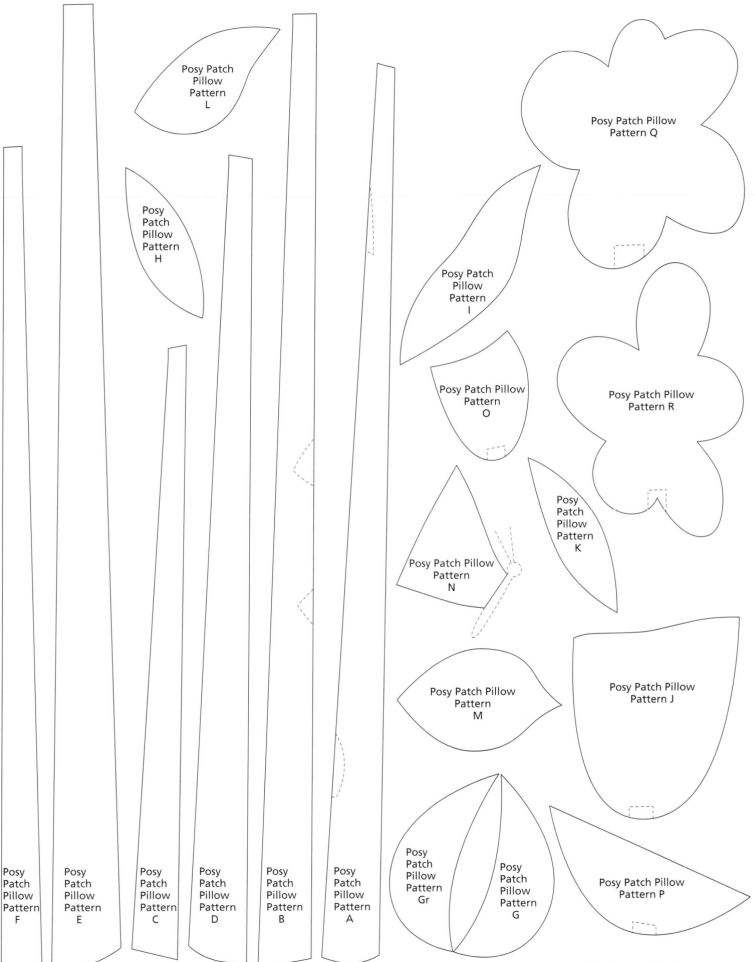

Posy Patch Pillow Pattern L

Posy Patch Pillow Pattern H

Posy Patch Pillow Pattern Q

Posy Patch Pillow Pattern I

Posy Patch Pillow Pattern O

Posy Patch Pillow Pattern R

Posy Patch Pillow Pattern K

Posy Patch Pillow Pattern N

Posy Patch Pillow Pattern M

Posy Patch Pillow Pattern J

Posy Patch Pillow Pattern F

Posy Patch Pillow Pattern E

Posy Patch Pillow Pattern C

Posy Patch Pillow Pattern D

Posy Patch Pillow Pattern B

Posy Patch Pillow Pattern A

Posy Patch Pillow Pattern Gr

Posy Patch Pillow Pattern G

Posy Patch Pillow Pattern P

patterns

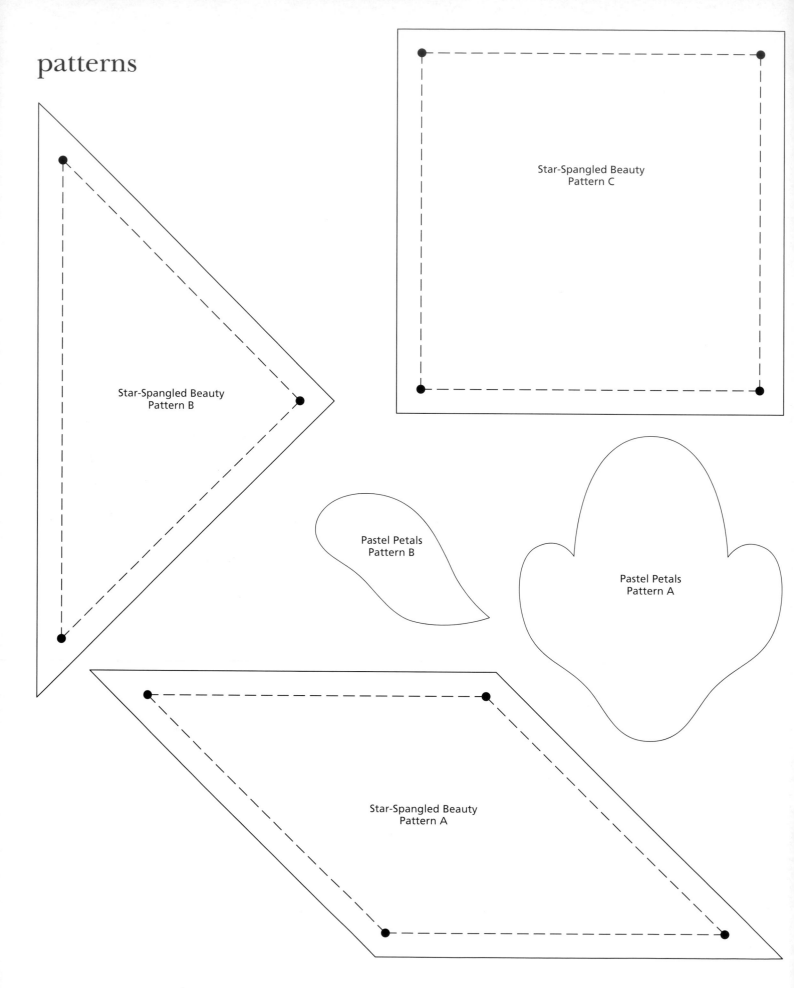

Star-Spangled Beauty
Pattern B

Star-Spangled Beauty
Pattern C

Pastel Petals
Pattern B

Pastel Petals
Pattern A

Star-Spangled Beauty
Pattern A

Pastel Petals
Full-Size Pattern Placement Diagram

patterns

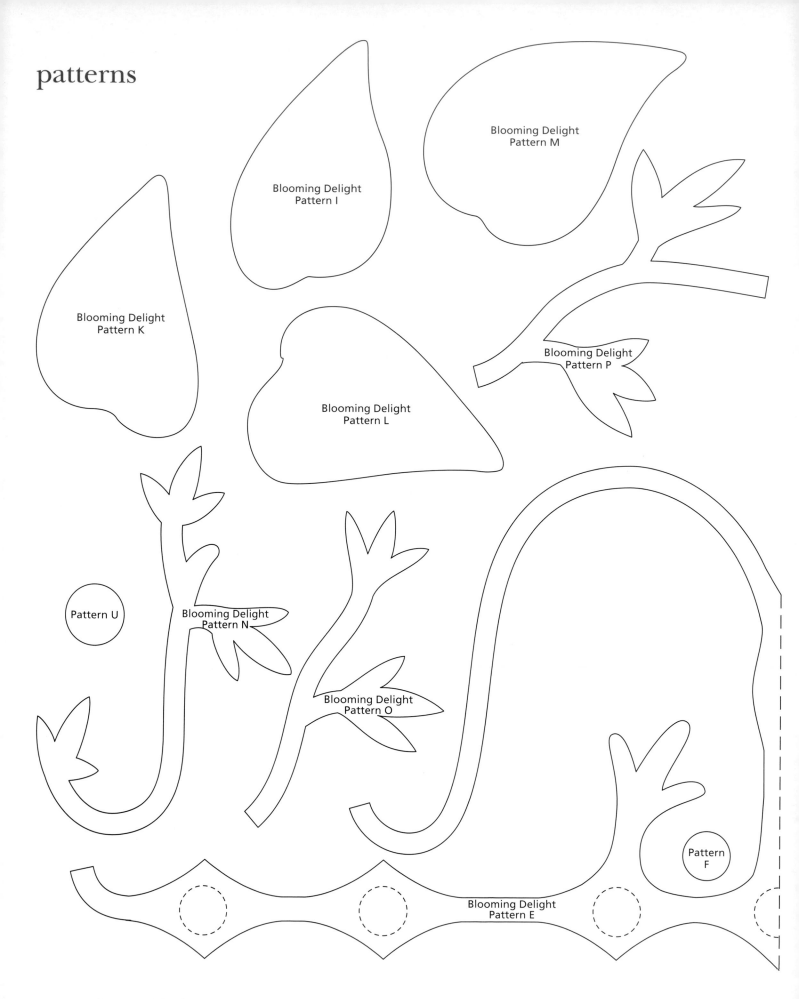

Blooming Delight
Pattern I

Blooming Delight
Pattern M

Blooming Delight
Pattern K

Blooming Delight
Pattern L

Blooming Delight
Pattern P

Pattern U

Blooming Delight
Pattern N

Blooming Delight
Pattern O

Pattern
F

Blooming Delight
Pattern E

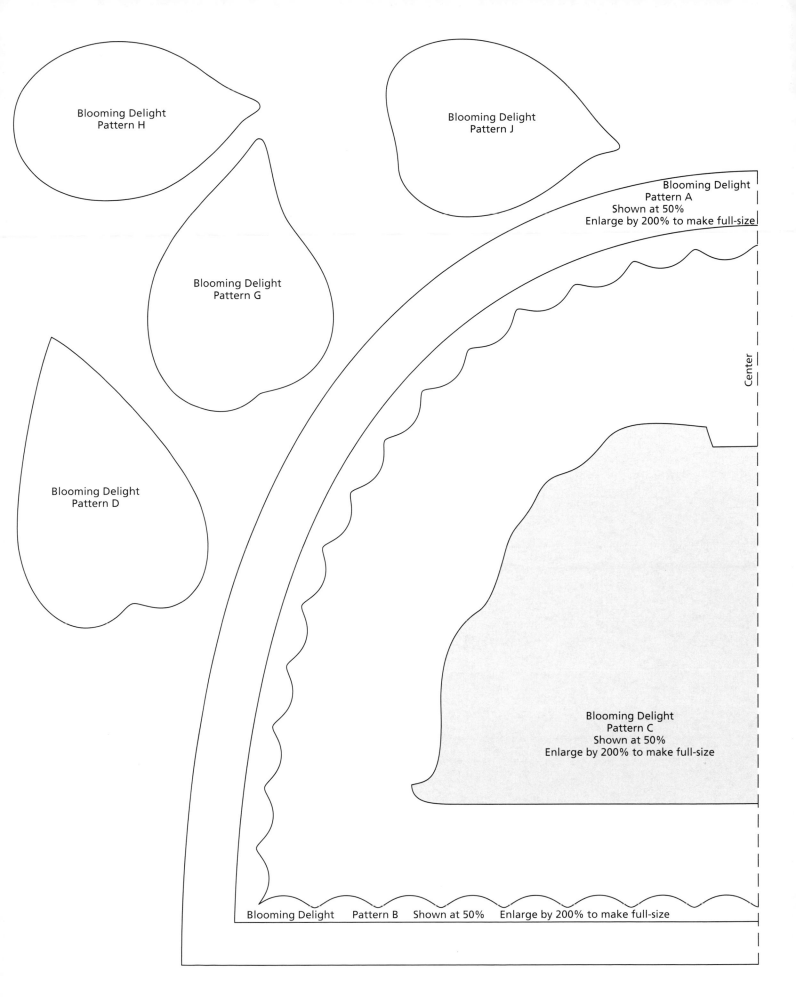

Blooming Delight
Pattern H

Blooming Delight
Pattern J

Blooming Delight
Pattern A
Shown at 50%
Enlarge by 200% to make full-size

Blooming Delight
Pattern G

Center

Blooming Delight
Pattern D

Blooming Delight
Pattern C
Shown at 50%
Enlarge by 200% to make full-size

Blooming Delight   Pattern B   Shown at 50%   Enlarge by 200% to make full-size

patterns

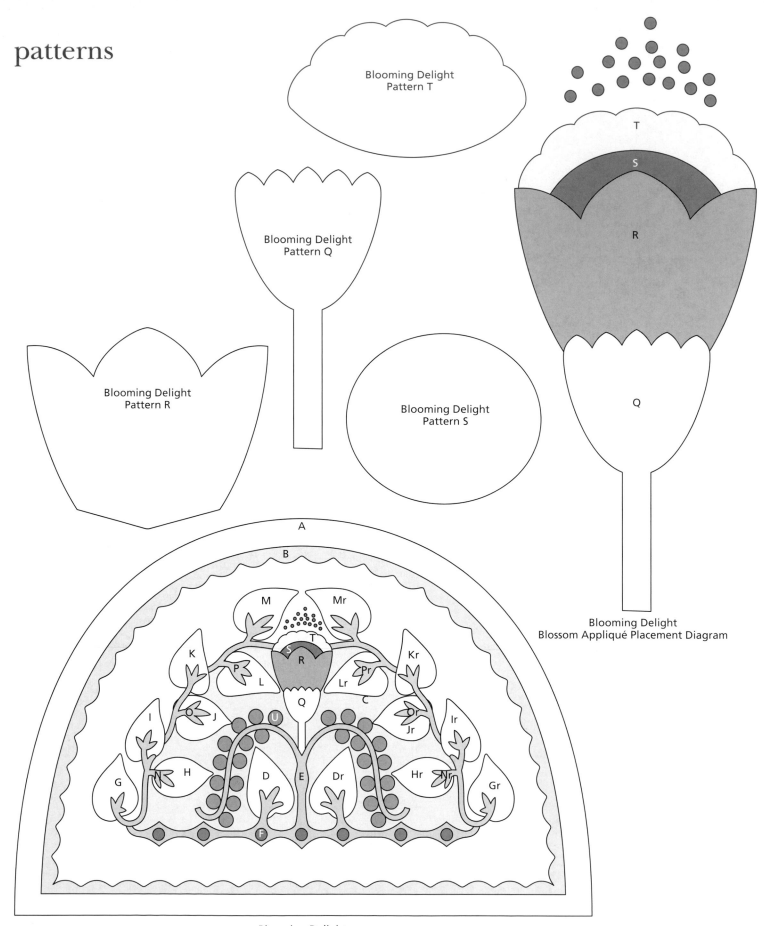

Blooming Delight
Pattern T

Blooming Delight
Pattern Q

Blooming Delight
Pattern R

Blooming Delight
Pattern S

Blooming Delight
Blossom Appliqué Placement Diagram

Blooming Delight
Appliqué Placement Diagram

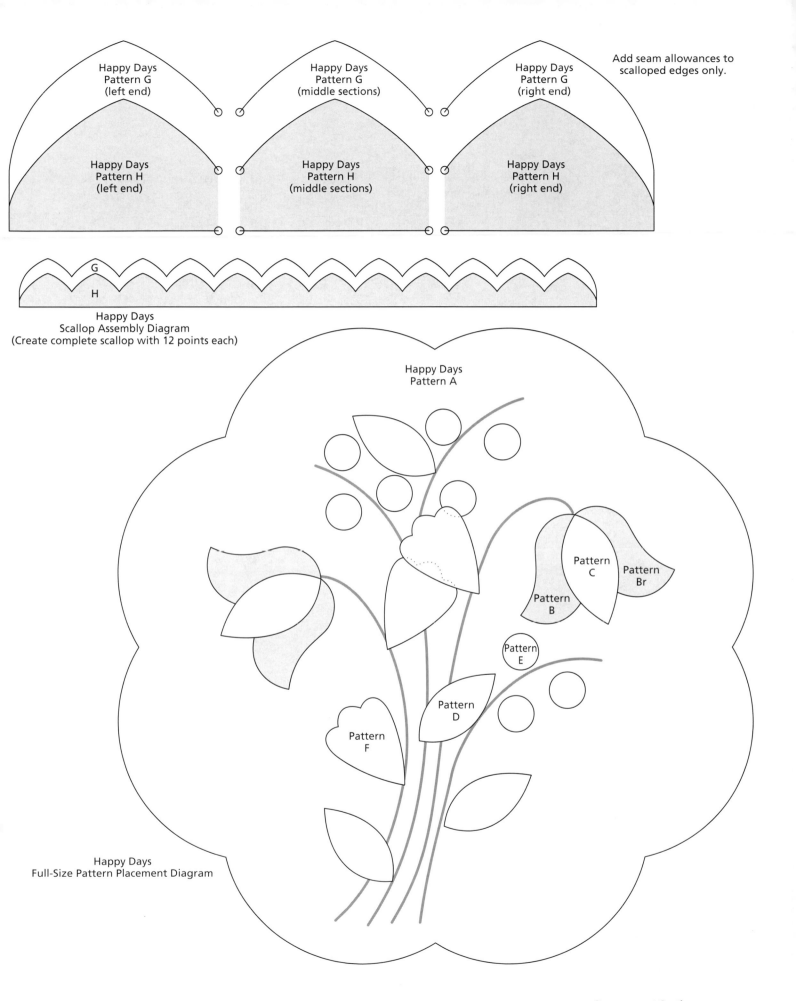

Happy Days
Pattern G
(left end)

Happy Days
Pattern G
(middle sections)

Happy Days
Pattern G
(right end)

Add seam allowances to
scalloped edges only.

Happy Days
Pattern H
(left end)

Happy Days
Pattern H
(middle sections)

Happy Days
Pattern H
(right end)

G

H

Happy Days
Scallop Assembly Diagram
(Create complete scallop with 12 points each)

Happy Days
Pattern A

Pattern
C

Pattern
Br

Pattern
B

Pattern
E

Pattern
D

Pattern
F

Happy Days
Full-Size Pattern Placement Diagram

Better Homes and Gardens®
Creative Collection™

Director, Editorial Administration
Michael L. Maine
Editor-in-Chief
Beverly Rivers
Executive Editor
Karman Wittry Hotchkiss

| Editorial Manager | Art Director |
| Ann Blevins | Don Nickell |

Copy Chief
Mary Heaton
Editorial Assistant
Lori Eggers
Contributing Graphic Designer
Barbara J. Gordon
Contributing Copy Editor
Lisa Flyr
Contributing Proofreader
Angela Ingle

American Patchwork & Quilting™
Executive Editor
Heidi Kaisand
Senior Editor
Jennifer Keltner
Art Director
Melissa Gansen-Beauchamp
Editors
Diane Yanney
Mary Helen Schiltz
Graphic Designer
Mary-Beth Majewski
Editorial Assistant
Mary Irish

Vice President, Publishing Director
William R. Reed

| Group Publisher | Steve Levinson |
| Senior Marketing Manager | Suzy Johnson |

CORPORATION
Chairman and CEO
William T. Kerr

In Memoriam
E. T. Meredith III (1933-2003)

Publishing Group President
Stephen M. Lacy
Magazine Group President
Jack Griffin

Copyright © 2004 by Meredith Corporation,
Des Moines, Iowa. All rights reserved.
Printed in the U.S.A.

credits

PHOTOGRAPHERS

Anderson, Craig: 9 bottom right; 11 bottom; 24 top left and center; 26 top; 33 bottom; 43 bottom; 49; 54 bottom right; 55 top; 59 top right; 60 top; 72 bottom left; 74 top left to right and middle; 76 top; 91; 95; 98 top; 103; 104; 107; 110; 115; 116; 119; 123; 124; 125

Cameron, Marcia: 12 top left; 16 top and bottom right; 18 bottom; 19 right; 20 bottom right; 21 bottom; 24 top right; 28 left; 31 bottom left and right; 37 bottom; 43 top; 44 bottom left and right; 47 bottom left; 58 middle left to middle right; 59 top left; 64 bottom; 65 top

Hedrich, Jim/Hedrich-Blessing: 75 right; 78

Hopkins Associates: 34 right; 39; 52 bottom; 61 top; 66 right

Little, Scott: 23; 41 top; 42; 73 top

Struse, Perry: 7; 9 top; 13; 17; 20 top right; 21 top; 25 top; 29; 30; 35; 36; 37 top right; 40 bottom right; 45; 46; 48 bottom right; 51; 54 top right; 57; 62 top; 68 bottom left; 71; 81; 83; 84; 85; 89; 92; 97; 101; 105; 109; 112; 117; 120; 127

Struse, Steve: 8; 12 bottom left and right; 15; 48 top; 53 top; 69 top right; 77 top right; 79 top

Wells, Jeff: 26 bottom

PROJECT QUILTERS AND FINISHERS

Field Daisies and Tulip Pillows
Ruth A. Smith
Windmill Quilt
Dorothy Faidley and
Kathleen M. Williams (piecing and binding)
Monica Hofer (quilting)
Blooming Delight
Mary Pepper
Pastel Petals
Patty Edmond
Star Diamond
Jan Bahr (piecing and binding)
Sally Terry (quilting)
Eight-Point All-Over
Kathleen M. Williams
Geometric Puzzle
Judy Sohn (piecing)

Dawn Cavanaugh (quilting and binding)
Posy Patch
Randall Parkin
Star-Spangled Beauty
Jill Reber (piecing and binding)
Anne Henter (quilting)

QUILT SOURCES

8 left: Barb Eckoff
8 top right: Jeananne Wright
10 Deborah Harding
12 right: Jim & Jill Reber
15 Gretchen Bearce
17 Xenia Cord/Legacy Quilts
21 Historic American Quilts
23 Marti Michell
26 Denver Art Museum
29 Marilyn Woodin/Woodin Wheel Antiques
30 Especially Lace
32 June Hall/Juneau-Douglas City Museum
33 Shirley McElderry
35 Marti Michell
36 Susan Miller
41 Shirley S. Sawyer
44 bottom left: Darlene Zimmerman
46 Heidi Kaisand
48 Lori Rees
53 Merikay Waldvogel
54 Susan Miller
55 Xenia Cord/Legacy Quilts
57 Laura Fisher/Antique Quilts & Americana
64 June Hall/Juneau-Douglas City Museum
66 bottom left: Merikay Waldvogel
67 Merikay Waldvogel
68 top left: Illinois State Museum
68 top right: Joyce Gross
68 bottom right: Jean Wishnick King
68 bottom left: Laura Fisher/Antique Quilts & Americana
69 Arlene Weimers Burgess
77 Heidi Kaisand
79 Heidi Kaisand

ADDITIONAL ITEMS

Cord, Xenia/Legacy Quilts: 12 top left; 24 top right; 43; 44 bottom right; 58 middle left to middle right; 59 top left to top right; 74 middle
McElderry, Shirley: 34 right
Miller, Susan: 11 bottom; 24 top left and center; 33 top; 37 top left and right; 54 top right; 60 top; 74 top left to right; 80 middle
Perry, Rosalind Webster: 19 left
Schroeder, Meredith/American Quilter's Society: 73 bottom right
Ver Mehren, Dick: 54 left
Waldvogel, Merikay: 50; 66 top left; 67 bottom right; 69 bottom